OLD ENGLISH
HOUSEHOLD LIFE

FIG. I.—INGLE NOOK, WELSH FARMSTEAD.

OLD ENGLISH HOUSEHOLD LIFE

Some account of Cottage objects and Country Folk

By

GERTRUDE JEKYLL

B. T. Batsford Ltd., London & Sydney

PREFACE
To the First Edition

IN the year 1904 the present writer, whose life had been passed in the south-west corner of Surrey, was the author of a book entitled " Old West Surrey." It was a record of the remembrance of the ways of the old country people and the things they used, especially those connected with fire and light. As the interest was chiefly local it went out of print, but, as time passes, the subject acquires a renewed value, and it was thought well that some of the illustrations and the subject matter of a part of the text, should be incorporated in the present book, with other material more or less allied ; and, though much of it concerns the home counties, that its scope should not be restricted to these but should have a wider range.

A number of the illustrations of the present book are reproductions from that remarkable work, Pyne's " Microcosm," published just a hundred years ago—before any of the present day disturbing influences were at work. For some of the others I am indebted to the kindness of the proprietors of " Country Life," and to them also for permission to reprint an article on the construction of the five barred gate. My thanks are also due to Dr. Collie and Miss Eckenstein for some examples from their remarkable collections of waggon horse brasses. Acknowledgment is also due to the journal of the Sussex Archæological Society, and for permission to reproduce objects in the Victoria and Albert Museum to the Board of Education. The provenance of the photographs is acknowledged in the accompanying note.

GERTRUDE JEKYLL.

May, 1925.

First edition published in 1925
Re-issued in 1933
New edition 1975

ISBN 0 7134 2983 6

Printed and bound in Great Britain by
Redwood Burn Limited
Trowbridge & Esher
for the publishers B. T. Batsford Ltd.,
4 Fitzhardinge St., London W1H 0AH
and 23 Cross St., Brookvale, NSW 2100, Australia

CONTENTS.

NOTE OF ACKNOWLEDGMENT.

My thanks are due to the owners of collections who have kindly placed much material at my disposal, especially Mr. John H. Every, of Lewes ; many illustrations have been photographed from his delightful series of old country objects. Mr. Godwin King has kindly permitted us to photograph the interiors and fittings of the Priests' House, West Hoathly (figs. 4, 114-115). A number of subjects are included from my own collection, now at the Guildford Museum, and figs. 28, 31, 36c, 39, 43, 61, 93, 153, 236, and 265 (the last four paintings) are from the collections at the Victória and Albert Museum. The provenance of the other photographs is as follows :—B. Ward Thompson, Esq., figs. 1, 14, and 207 ; Messrs. Taunt & Co., of Oxford, figs. 5, 158, 175, 209, 211, 215, 250, and 264 ; Horace Dan, Esq., fig. 9 ; the successors of the late Mr. Kevis, of Petworth, fig. 8 ; Percy Bedford, Esq., figs. 10, 178, and 206 ; the Rev. F. W. Cobb, Rector of Alfold, fig. 11 ; Mr. G. Hepworth, Brighouse, Yorks, fig. 13 ; The Carron Co., fig. 53 ; the late Mr. W. Galsworthy Davie, figs. 54, 94, 117, 119, 120, 122-128, 130, 133, 210, 212, 214, 216, 234, 237, 239, 240, 255-256, 266-268, and 276 ; R. Cox, Esq. (Lincoln), figs. 90 and 194 ; Frank Leney, Esq., of the Folk Museum, Norwich, fig. 30 ; F. H. Crossley, Esq., figs. 134, 172, 184, 269, and 275 ; Messrs. R. Wilkinson & Son, of Trowbridge, fig. 167 ; the late Mr. W. Pouncy, of Dorchester, figs. 173, 193, and 262 ; the late Sir Benjamin Stone, figs. 183, 204, and 277 ; W. F. Wastell, Esq., figs. 188 and 199 ; the Rev. E. A. Godson, Shropshire, fig. 200 ; W. Marriott Dodson, Esq., figs. 189, 190, and 274 ; Miss L. Eckenstein, figs. 225-226 ; the British Museum, figs. 177 and 234 ; Dr. Frank Collie, figs. 227-231 ; Messrs. Frith & Co., Reigate, figs. 249, 251-253; A. O. Collard, Esq., fig. 174. Thanks are also due to the Cambridge University Press for permission to reproduce fig. 116 from C. F. Innocent's " Development of Building Construction." To the kindness of " Country Life," I owe figs. 118, 150-2, 156-7, 159, and 237. Messrs. Longmans have kindly supplied the electros of a number of subjects from my work on " Old West Surrey," and some illustrations have been reproduced from the material at the British Museum, collected by the late Mr. J. Romilly Allen, F.S.A., from the " Reliquary and Illustrated Archæologist." To the Photochrom Co. we are indebted for fig. 148, and for the view of Farnham (fig. 217) to the Bodleian Library. The illustrations of Branks, figs. 255-9, are from an article in " Building News," published in 1882. Figure 263 is from the Sussex Archæological Society's Proceedings, and is included by consent of the Society.

FIG. 2.—SEVEN-FOOT OAK TABLE.

FIG. 3.—OAK CHEST OF DRAWERS.

FIG. 4.—AN INTERIOR WITH OLD FITTINGS. THE PRIEST'S HOUSE, WEST HOATHLY, SUSSEX.
Vide also Figs. 114 and 115.

INTRODUCTION.

THE last sixty years have seen so many changes in the ways of living among the rural working people of the country, that it is well to have some written remembrance of the older and, in many respects, better ways that are within the memory of people still living. The changes have been more rapid in the neighbourhood of the greater urban centres. If we take as a group the home counties, we shall find that in all but the more remote districts, such as one five or six miles from a railway station, the old grace and kindliness of speech and manner are gone. This is a grievous loss, and it is accompanied by so much else that is regrettable that it is a pleasure and relief to get down to the West Country, where the people are still kindly of manner and show a charming friendliness. Their way of living and outlook on life had gone on almost unchanged for generations, and, except when specially hard times came, as in the forties of the nineteenth century, they were content and happy. Their interests were centred in their place of dwelling and daily labour, and only extended to what was doing and happening within a radius of a very few miles. Special industries were connected with certain districts ; of these, only a few now remain, such as the chair-making at High Wycombe in Buckinghamshire, established there because beech wood was in plenty ; the straw-plaiting in Bedfordshire, the making of wooden clogs near the industrial midlands ; lace-making in Devon and one or two other centres. Potteries for common ware, where suitable clay is found, are in some places still working, though in many others they have ceased to exist because of easier communication with the great stoneware and porcelain works in Staffordshire. Windmills may be said to be dead and many water mills are dead or dying. So it is also in the appurtenances of cottage and farmhouse ; the strong, simple and beautiful furniture, for the most part of oak, admirably adapted to the needs of the home, that had been in these dwellings for generations, has now been replaced by something pretentious and shoddy. As Mr. Laurence Binyon has recently written : " Alas ! the fine shapes that marked our old handicrafts have long ago disappeared ; the domestic utensils and furniture that gave dignity by their fine simplicity of form and careful workmanship to country cottages have been driven out by dull products of cheapening commerce, things whose making gave no pleasure to those who made them, and whose use gives none to those who use them. Admirable specimens of our old crafts exist, but scattered about, and in remote places for the most part. It is to the old models that those who are now trying to reawaken beauty in the homely arts should turn for guidance. We need not reproduce old forms with servility, but if we wish to preserve an English character, we shall look long and carefully at those works which bring down to us the tradition of those who wrought so well for our ancestors."*

The change would appear to have come about with the increase in the use of steam machinery. Articles that were once made singly and by one man throughout, are now turned out by the hundred or thousand, and the work is sub-divided, so that no one man has the satisfaction of seeing the labour of his hands completed and well done. This is one of the most serious losses of our times, for a man's work should be to him not a matter of toil only, but something that is of interest all through, and of this pleasure his life has been robbed by modern conditions. In the old days, if a rush light holder or any simple implement for the house was wanted, or a hoe for field or garden, it was made by the nearest smith. A mousetrap or moletrap that we now buy at the ironmonger's was made of wood at home. Everything tended to give interest to hand work, and to stimulate invention and its adaptation to simple needs.

Another of the debasing influences may be attributed to trade competition, which brings into being quantities of things that are of no utility or beauty, that are merely made to sell and are got up with a kind of superficial attractiveness.

It is a pleasure to think back in imagination a hundred years, and to consider how good a thing it must have been to go into the business part of any town and see what was then shown in the shop windows— everything for some definite use and with only such added grace of form as was consistent with utility. It is the same kind of satisfaction that one feels in seeing the wares in the market place of a foreign town ; fruit and vegetables, crockery and simple clothing, wooden shoes and peasant tools, all coming straight from the producer.

* Introduction to *Old English Metalwork, by W. Twopeny,* 1904.

It is evident, both from the teachings of history and the experience of the present day, that country life has an ingrained attraction for the English race, and in spite of the thrall of commercialism, this tendency continues to show itself, especially at abnormal times such as those in the recent war. The workers in the industrial cities of England have usually either come from the country themselves or can trace a rural origin a generation or two back, and the majority of English people look with longing to the country side and cherish the wish to end their days in its retirement. There is no doubt that this influence has persisted during many generations from the strain of the Saxons, who ignored the Roman villa settlements and made their " hams " or village clearings in the woods. Many feel that town life is not truly satisfying, and if there is much to deplore in modern conditions, there is at least a very real and widespread inclination towards the simplicity of country life. Even if the recurrent sternness of economic conditions is again barring doors that seemed to open after the war, the desire for the country must be regarded as a basic factor of English life. But the whole of the outlook is not gloomy. As a heritage of war there are evidences of a considerable brightening of village life, and much hopeful promise in the training homes and industrial centres for partly disabled soldiers.

It has, perhaps, only recently been realised that household life of the seventeenth and eighteenth centuries, before the industrial revolution, stands at the end of a long continued tradition, going back to neolithic days. Nothing is so enduring as the life and work of the countryman ; he works to supply human primitive wants and he must needs base his work on primitive methods. Thus the old types of objects illustrated in this book have their roots in prehistoric days. These cottage objects and country appliances are almost always simple, beautiful and appropriate to their uses, and the variety and ingenuity of devices is remarkable ; they have the qualities of real craftsmanship and are, it may be claimed, in the true sense of the word artistic. There is an instinctive feeling for form, and they are not only adapted by centuries of experience to their practical uses, but are also beautifully expressive of the native materials from which they are fashioned. There is, as a rule, little ornament, and that is concentrated at one or two points. The tradition of simple craftsmanship expressed in the household objects of the seventeenth and eighteenth centuries persisted well into the nineteenth century, and it may be noted that traditional craftsmanship may yet be seen in the waggon builders' art, of which Mr. C. H. B. Quennell is anxious to record examples. The tradition may be seen in the lines of the cart and also the elaborate chamfering and gay painting. Another local industry which still flourishes is the turning of chair legs in the beech woods on the Chiltern Hills of Buckinghamshire and Oxfordshire. Traditional turning patterns are there reproduced by cottagers in sheds attached to the cottages, by means of a primitive pole lathe, and after being stacked to dry, the parts are fitted into chairs in the factories at High Wycombe. In some cases men work in a little hut in the woods, known as the " Bodger's shop." This is an interesting reversion to primitive conditions, only paralleled by the work of the charcoal burner.

It cannot be said that there is any hope of recapturing the traditional spirit by which these articles were made. It has vanished with the coming of totally new conditions, and attempts to revive handcraftsmanship are often in the nature of exotic or hothouse plants. Nevertheless, it is possible that some day art and simplicity shall inspire the product of the machine, and fine work may once more flourish.

It is at least a cause for thankfulness that there has been a revival of domestic architecture in England, especially in regard to smaller country houses. Some qualities of the old work have reappeared, not through slavish imitation, but through a reversion to something of its ancient spirit. Consider the difference between the better type of small country house to-day and that of fifty years ago ; there is a feeling for proportion, a desire for the use of local materials, a wish that the work of man may harmonise with its surroundings—a happy reaction from the blight of bad building that descended on the country in the middle of the nineteenth century.

The late Mr. J. Romilly Allen, F.S.A., collected a large amount of material, now in the National Collections, towards a history of Human Appliances. It is intensely interesting to observe how humanity has devised means of meeting its primary needs, and there is often a similarity in the simple and ingenious means of accomplishing household tasks, traceable in the products of different races in widely-severed lands over great periods of time. It is, of course, to be expected that the old household appliances of Scotland, Ireland and Colonial America should parallel those of England, with just a touch of local modification. But all over the world, primitive peoples living near to nature seem to have arrived at results much alike in the case of objects of

FIG. 5.—THE WINDMILL, LACEY GREEN, BUCKS.

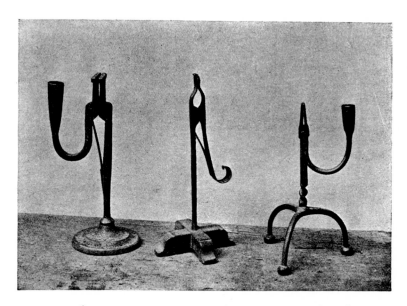

FIG 6.—RUSHLIGHT HOLDERS (THE TALLEST $9\frac{1}{2}$ IN.).

8

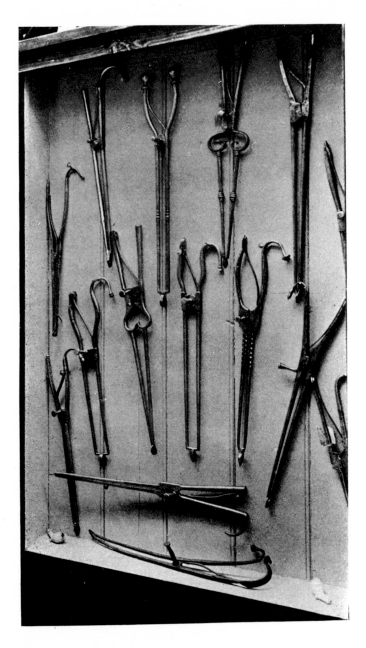

FIG. 7.—BRAND TONGS.

For picking up a fragment of live wood or peat, for lighting a pipe or rushlight.   One
handle has usually a curled end for hanging up.   The projecting stud is a tobacco stopper.

From the Every Collection, Lewes.

the hearth, or of vessels for cooking and storing, or agricultural implements.

It is a matter for regret that no really adequate record or collection of English village craftsmanship exists. The great city museums are more concerned with fine works of art, and such objects as have survived are mostly scattered in small quantities in local museums and private collections. Some of these museums, where there has been a local industry, such as the Sussex Ironwork, are well equipped, but many have little, hidden among foreign and often irrelevant material, and it is lamentable to think of what has been destroyed in the past fifty years. Some local residents have, on their own initiative, made collections of objects and devices illustrating the past country life of their district. Such efforts—like those shown in the excellent collections of the three generations of the Horne family at Leyburn in Wensleydale, Yorkshire, the Priests' House, West Hoathly, here illustrated (Figs. 4, 114, 115), or of Mr. J. H. Every at Lewes, which has been drawn on for illustration in these pages, cannot be too highly commended, and are worthy of imitation. Many who live in the country can help by recording the fast passing features of local life and by collecting examples of vanished craftsmanship. The value of such material to future generations is not to be estimated. There is support for the movement started by the Society for the Protection of Ancient Buildings, to stop the soulless destruction of old cottages, and the same good work is being carried out practically by Mr. Harold Falkner and Mr. Borelli at Farnham ; let us hope that this may be extended to the fittings and objects which these cottages contained. The folk songs and tunes of the past are to some extent preserved to us ; let us not lose entirely the setting of household life in the English country.

Limited as is the scope of this book, it is hoped that it may not be altogether inadequate as a record of a simple natural life and a charming local craftsmanship which has now died out, possibly for ever. The scheme of the work is simple. Starting with the hearth as the centre of the family life, it reviews the numerous objects connected with the fire and cooking. Then we pass to appliances for giving light ; furniture and ornaments ; pictures ; needlework, &c., and from there to the implements connected with farming, travel, &c., which in the wider sense may claim to be reckoned as products of English household life.

Conditions of publication have in the last few years raised great obstacles to the provision of a more detailed record, and yet nothing could be finer than a really systematic illustrated record of the products of English rural life that is gone.

It has been found difficult to describe the scope of the book by any title that would be at the same time comprehensive and succinct. As will be seen, it concerns objects of daily use rather than any of the wider aspects of life.

PUBLISHER'S NOTE

One or two of the sections in this book also appear in Gertrude Jekyll's *Old West Surrey*. As both books are now being re-issued, it seems best to publish them in exactly the form in which they were prepared by the Author.

December, 1974

FIG. 8 —AT LODSWORTH, WEST SUSSEX.

FIG. 9.——BEX FARM, KENT.

FIG. 10.—COTTAGE FIREPLACE AND OVEN, WIGMORE, HEREFORDSHIRE.

FIG. 11.—THE OLD FOLKS BY THE FIRE, SURREY.

I.

THE EVOLUTION OF THE FIREPLACE.

IT is interesting to trace the development of the fireplace from the earliest times of which we have records or remains in our islands. The fireplace and chimney as we now have them were unknown in ordinary dwelling houses until the sixteenth century and were only then beginning to be general. Some such fireplaces were only in the greater castles and palaces, and even in some of these buildings still existing, the ancient fireplace, as at Penshurst, remains in the middle of the floor of the great hall, with its heavy iron coupled andirons to hold up the logs. The alternative to this was an iron brazier for burning charcoal or peat. The smoke found its way out as it could, usually through a hole in the roof or by interstices in thatch or tiling, or any openings as of doors or windows. The timbers of the roof became coated with soot, and in the case of a leaky roof of thatch the wet streamed down laden with black. Though the smoke of wood or peat is more tolerable than that of coal, yet the conditions of living must, to our modern ideas, have been full of discomfort. They were the same, in fact, differing only in degree, as those of the dwellers in the circular huts of the ancient Britons of which there are remains, for then also the hearth for the fire was in the centre and the sleeping places all round ; the sleepers lying with their feet to the fire. Even in the great hall of the castle the arrangement was the same, of a central fire and a general sleeping place surrounding it.

The most primitive form of fireplace may even now be seen in the Orkney and Shetland Islands, where it consists of a central hearth and a rising lump of stone, slightly hollowed in one face, that forms a backing to the fire. An iron hanger to hold a pot is suspended from above (Fig. 12).

The first advance towards a chimney was in the later part of the thirteenth century, when the hole in the roof was covered with open boarding in the form that is still known as louvres ; they were made of horizontal slats of wood, fixed apart and set diagonally in order to throw off the wet, and roofed in at the top. Later, when these were of some size they were treated architecturally and formed handsome features on the building. Several good examples remain, and though they are no longer needed for their original purpose, they are treasured for their architectural value.

When built chimneys came to be general, the fireplace was still of a very simple form. As wood was the usual fuel, the only alternative being either deep-bedded or surface peat, the place for the fire was built wide and deep, often large enough for stout oak seats to be built in on each side. In Sussex and Surrey and the home counties generally, it was called a "down" hearth. There are still some in use in remote and moorland districts, and very pleasant they are on winter evenings when fuel is in plenty and when the enclosed space of the wide chimney opening is continued into the room by an opposite pair of long, high-backed settles, and sometimes by a curtain that draws right round.

Fig. 12.—A "REREDOS" FROM THE SHETLAND ISLES.

It was frequent, in the region of the iron foundries of the Weald of Sussex, as well as farther north, for the cottage hearth to have a flooring of a thick cast-iron plate with a course of brick or stone supporting it to right and left, leaving a space in the middle under the hottest of the fire. Whether this space was actually used for baking seems uncertain, but in any case it was a good place for warming plates or keeping food hot.

Baking was done on the down hearth by laying an earthen pan bottom up over the loaf or cake and heaping hot ashes all round. In these fires it was usual to have one large heavy log at the back, and it might be weeks before this was burnt through. The ashes were left in a goodly heap, and there were always in the morning a few bits with fire still smouldering that could be blown up into flame with the bellows. Meanwhile, the whole hearth kept warm and was in a favourable state for encouraging the new morning's fire.

In farm houses and many of the better class of cottage there was a brick oven for baking, shown in Figs. 91, 92. It was built with a brick floor and arched like a tunnel and had an iron door. A faggot was set alight within and when it was burnt and the ashes raked out it was right for baking. Old people will remember the little atoms of charcoal that stuck to the bottom of the loaf.

The illustrations show the general development of the farm or cottage fireplace. At Fig. 8 we see the simple " down " fire in a farm house in West Sussex. The fire is on the brick hearth, level with the room floor ; it was more often raised a step, which is better both for draught and for getting at the cooking. There is a plain iron fire-back and a pair of cup-dogs. The iron pot is slung over the fire by a long hook leading to a hanger from a chimney crane ; an oak beam stretches across, carried by the jambs to right and left. Above is a moulded shelf and a spit-rack, both of later date than the original building, but still of respectable age, for they go well back into the eighteenth century. A grand old spit rests upon the rack, evidently an old family possession ; it is kept bright by the careful housewife ; the hooks at the backs of the cup-dogs show where it rested in cooking the great joints of meat. On the shelf are more family treasures ; three pairs of brass candlesticks and a brass mortar, and beyond them, on the wall, a pair of brand tongs. To the left are the sheet iron candlebox and the bellows. A seat is notched into the wall on the right.

The next illustration (Fig. 9) shows a Kentish back kitchen. In this case the hearth is raised ; the fire has a good cast-iron back, probably from the old Sussex ironworks. There is an iron plate at the bottom and an arrangement of loose fire bricks and iron bars. The fire is mainly of wood, but a heap of coke or clinker at the side shows that other fuel was also used. The brick oven is to the right ; its iron door with two handles stands against the wall below.

The next example, from Herefordshire (Fig. 10), shows the older large space contracted by a wall one brick thick to the right, and a built-up fire-place with a wrought-iron front of three bars. It is interesting to note in this ironwork, a recollection of fire dogs, in the slightly swan-necked upright ends, capped by small balls. The iron pot still swings from above, showing that there must be a firebar across the chimney.

A further development, this time from Yorkshire (Fig. 13), shows a fire-place of later date built into the smaller width now usual, but with the fire still on the hearth on an iron plate with a space underneath, much like what is usual in the older cottages in Sussex ; but the advance is in having something of the nature of an oven or boiler with a moulded cast-iron front, though from the picture itself its use in this case is obscure. The fire is of peat. This fireplace may have been built in from an older and wider one ; the cupboard door on the right showing that there must be a recess within, that would be accounted for by the remainder of the older and wider hearth-place. Another example from Yorkshire (Fig. 14), with a cast-iron fronted oven, shows a clinging to the older ways, for there are still the chimney crane and a number of different hangers. The mistress is here baking a cake on a peat fire ; the pan has an iron lid on which she has put a number of pieces of glowing peat, thus giving heat above and below, after the French cook's manner of braising with *feu dessus-dessous*.

Another picture, from Wales (frontispiece), shows a nearer fore-runner of the modern kitchener, with a coal fire, an oven on one side and a boiler on the other. Even in this the crane still survives and holds the kettle. It was an error in taste to cover the arching beam with wall paper, but probably its ancient roughness offended the house-proud sensibilities of the good housewife. The chimney shelf holds a handsome teapot, a cake mould, and some brass candlesticks. Suspended from the joists are two parallel bars, that, had they been in a back kitchen or some other cooler place than just before the fire would have been taken for a bacon rack ; here they are no doubt used for airing sheets. On the wall of the recess to the right hang a variety of kitchen implements, all beautifully kept—tongs and shovel, frying-pan, chopper, meat saw, toasting fork, strainers and skimmers ; also some of the master's gear— bridle bits and a large hooked spring balance.

FIG. 14.—A YORKSHIRE FARM FIRE. CAKE BAKING IN
A COVERED PAN WITH BURNING PEAT ON COVER.

FIG. 13.—A TURF FIREPLACE IN A YORKSHIRE
FARM-HOUSE.

FIG. 15.—RUSHES DIPPED AND LAID IN BARK.

FIG. 16.—GREASE PANS.

II.

COTTAGE CANDLELIGHT.

WE who are accustomed to strike a match when we want a light can hardly realise what a difficult job it was a century and a half ago. We now have brilliant and clean light from electricity; for less than a hundred years before, we had all sorts of lamps fed with vegetable or mineral oil. In the early days of the eighteenth century candles were the only means of having artificial light, even in the best houses. But in cottages, until about the year 1830, or even perhaps later, the only artificial illuminant other than the firelight was from the rush lights that were made at home. In full summer time when the rushes were at their best, they were collected by women and children and prepared for drying. In the words of an old woman who told me all about it :— "You peels away the rind from the peth, leavin' only a little strip of rind, and when the rushes is dry you dips 'em in the grease, keepin' 'em well under ; and my mother she always laid hers to dry in a bit of hollow bark. Mutton fat's the best, it dries hardest." It is interesting to compare this first-hand description with that written by William Cobbett, and published in his " Cottage Economy," in 1822 :—" My grandmother, who lived to be pretty nearly ninety, never, I believe, burnt a candle in her house in her life. I know that I never saw one there and she, in a great measure, brought me up. She used to get the meadow-rushes, such as they tie the hop-shoots to the poles with. She cut them when they had attained their full substance, but were yet green. The rush, at this age, consists of a body of pith with a green skin on it. You cut off both ends of the rush and leave the prime part which, on an average, may be about a foot and a half long. Then you take off all the green skin, except for about a fifth part of the way round the pith. Thus it is a piece of pith, all but a little strip of skin in one part, all the way up, which, observe, is necessary to hold the pith together all the way along.

" The rushes being thus prepared, the grease is melted and put in a melted state into something that is as long as the rushes are. The rushes are put into the grease, soaked in it sufficiently, then taken out and laid in a bit of bark taken from a young tree, so as not to be too large. This bark is fixed up against the wall by a couple of straps put round it ; and there it hangs for the purpose of holding the rushes."

A still more detailed account of the making of rush lights is given by Gilbert White in one of the letters in his " History of Selborne." The letter is dated November, 1775. He says :—" The proper species of rush for this purpose seems to be the *juncus effusus,* or common soft rush, which is to be found in most moist pastures, by the sides of streams and under hedges. These rushes are in the best condition in the height of summer ; but may be gathered, so as to serve the purpose well, quite on to autumn. It would be needless to add that the largest and longest are best. Decayed labourers, women and children, make it their business to procure and prepare them. As soon as they are cut they must be flung into water and kept there, for otherwise they will dry and shrink and the peel will not run. At first a person would find it no easy matter to divest a rush of its peel or rind so as to leave one regular, narrow, even rib from top to bottom that may support the pith, but this, like other feats, soon becomes familiar even to children ; and we have seen an old woman, stone blind, performing this business with great dispatch, and seldom failing to strip them with the nicest regularity. When these *junci* are thus far prepared they must lie out on the grass to be bleached, and take the dew for some nights and afterwards be dried in the sun. Some address is required in dipping these rushes in the scalding fat or grease, but this knack also is to be attained by practice. The careful wife of an industrious Hampshire labourer obtains all her fat for nothing for she saves the scummings of her bacon pot for this use ; and if the grease abounds with salt she causes the salt to precipitate to the bottom by setting the scummings in a warm oven. Where hogs are not much in use, and especially by the seaside, the coarser animal oils will come very cheap. A pound of common grease may be procured for fourpence, and about six pounds of grease will dip a pound of rushes, and one pound of rushes may be bought for one shilling, so that a pound of rushes, medicated and ready for use, will cost three shillings. If men that keep bees will mix a little wax with the grease it will give it a consistency and render it more cleanly and make the rushes burn longer ; mutton suet would have the same effect. A good rush, which measured in length two feet four inches and a half, being minuted, burnt only three minutes short of an hour, and a rush of still greater length has been known to burn one hour and a quarter. These rushes give a good clear light. Watch-lights (coated with tallow), it is true, shed a dismal one,

FIG. 18.—CANDLE-BOX.

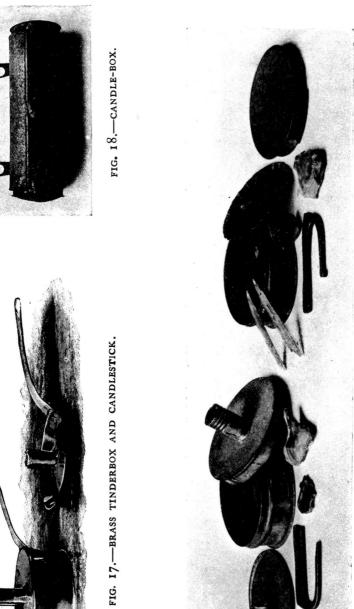

FIG. 17.—BRASS TINDERBOX AND CANDLESTICK.

FIG. 19.—IRON TINDERBOXES, STEELS, ETC.

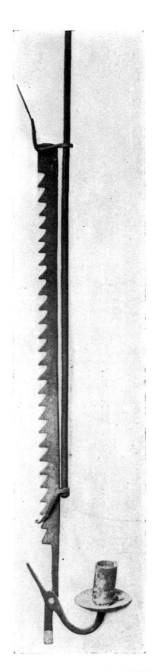

FIG. 20.—RUSHLIGHT IN HOLDER.   FIG. 21.—HANGING IRON   FIG. 22.—IRON CAND

CANDLESTICK.   STICK WITH SPIKE.

After Striking

Ready to Strike

FIG. 24.—STRIKE-A-LIGHT.

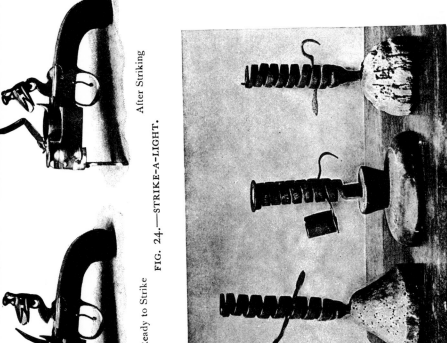

FIG. 25.—SPIRAL IRON CANDLESTICKS.

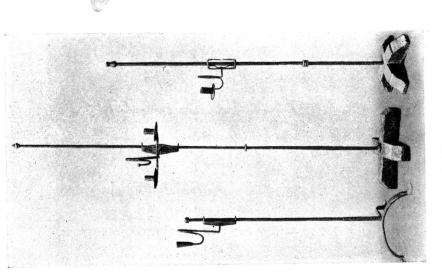

FIG. 23.—STANDING IRON RUSHLIGHT
AND CANDLE HOLDERS.

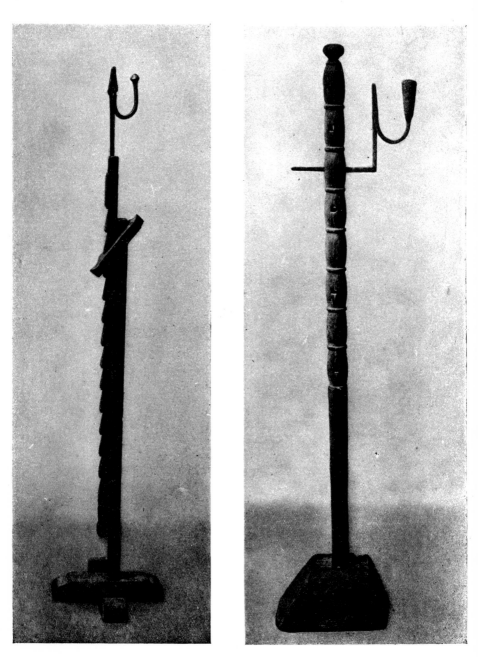

FIGS. 26, 27.—WOODEN STANDING RUSHLIGHT HOLDERS.

'darkness visible'; but then the wick of those have two ribs of the rind or peel to support the pith, while the wick of the dipped rush has but one. The two ribs are intended to impede the progress of the flame and make the candle last. In a pound of dry rushes, averdupois, which I caused to be weighed and numbered, we found upwards of one thousand six hundred individuals. Now suppose each of these burns one with another only half an hour, then a poor man will purchase eight hundred hours of light, a time exceeding thirty three entire days, for three shillings. According to this account, each rush before dippings costs one-thirty-third of a farthing, and one-eleventh afterwards. Thus a poor family will enjoy five and a half hours of comfortable light for a farthing. An experienced old housekeeper assures me that one pound and a half of rushes completely supplies his family the year round, since working people burn no candles in the long days, because they rise and go to bed by daylight. Little farmers use rushes much in the short days, both morning and evening, in the dairy and kitchen, but the very poor, who are always the worst economists, and, therefore, must continue very poor, buy a halfpenny candle every evening which, in their blowing, open rooms, does not burn much more than two hours. Thus they have only two hours' light for their money instead of eleven."

There are still to be found, or at any rate to be seen in local museums, the cast-iron grease pans or grease boats on three legs, the front legs worn short by much use in the fire (Fig. 16). I have never seen one large enough to take a rush eighteen inches long as described by Cobbett, but he is so accurate and his grandmother evidently such a keen and capable housewife that no doubt there was a grease pan of extra size among her household implements. In the pans of usual length the rush would have been passed through the grease slowly enough for it to imbibe its fill.

The only way of getting a light in the older days, other than by a live brand remaining in the ashes, was by the flint and steel and tinder box, illustrated on in Figs. 17 and 19. The tinder box was a round box four inches across and two inches deep, made of tinned sheet iron. The later made ones had a socket for a candle in the top of the lid and a ring handle so that they could be carried like a candlestick. Better ones were well made of brass with long handles, like those of the candlesticks known as the frying pan shape, which were commonly made of brass but also of silver. The tinder was in the bottom of the box; over it was the damper, a disk with a ring handle, and above this the flint and steel and one or two sulphur matches, which lifted out with the damper. The hook-shaped steel was made of a bit of good stuff, commonly of an old file. It was held over the fingers of the left hand and struck by the flint held in the right. A few strokes would bring a spark which fell on the tinder ; a little gentle blowing would partly ignite the tinder and the point of the sulphur match would come alight. The matches were thin slips of wood dipped in melted brimstone. Men working in the fields could, at a pinch, get a light by picking up a bit of flint and striking it on the back of a knife ; they carried a slip of touch paper in their pockets to act as tinder.

The tinder was made of any rags of cotton or linen—blue rags were mostly in favour. The rag was held in the fire with the tongs till it was well alight, then dropped into the tinder box and instantly quenched with the damper.

The first matches for general use that ignited by friction, such as we now have, but in a more primitive form, were made about the year 1838.

The iron holders for rush lights varied in form within certain limits, but the earliest consisted of an upright, spiked into a wooden block, ending at the top in one of the flattened jaws that held the rush, as seen in Fig. 20. The other jaw was movable, working on a loose rivet ; its free end curved down and up again as a convenient means of handling and ended in a knob heavy enough to keep the jaws close and the rush in position. In later examples, in place of the knob there was a small candle socket, and, later still, a more elaborate pattern with horizontal jaws and a spring to ensure fast holding. The sockets were for rush candles and the earlier forms of other candles dipped in tallow. The rush candles retained the rush as a wick, but were dipped several times in the grease so as to have a much thicker coating. Later, cotton wicks took the place of rushes, but the candles were still dipped. The moulded candles that we know came later, but still candle-making was for some time a home industry. The rush dips and the earlier tallow candles were kept in the sheet-iron candle-box (Fig. 18), whose shape shows its descent from the rounded piece of bark that held the more primitive greased rushes.

Many were the forms of candlesticks and their ways of adjustment. In the farm kitchen one with a ratchet arrangement would hang from a beam, another would have spikes at the back for driving into a post (Figs. 21 and 22), and there were a number of other variants showing things locally made to suit the need of the place. There was a curious kind with an open spiral twist of iron ; a thin piece of iron strap passing

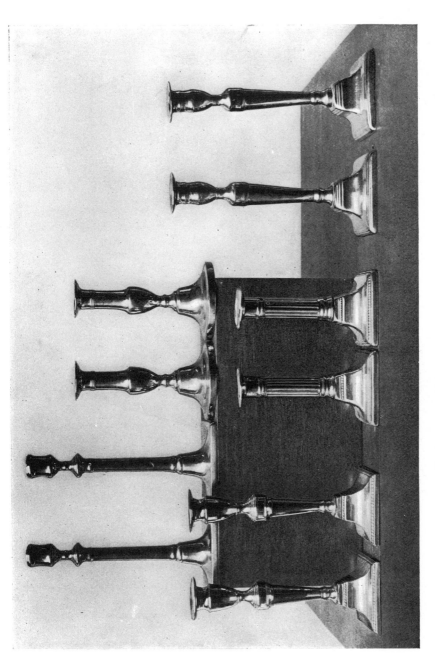

FIG. 28.—EIGHTEENTH CENTURY BRASS CANDLESTICKS.

FIG. 29 —CANDLESTICKS OF LATER DATE.

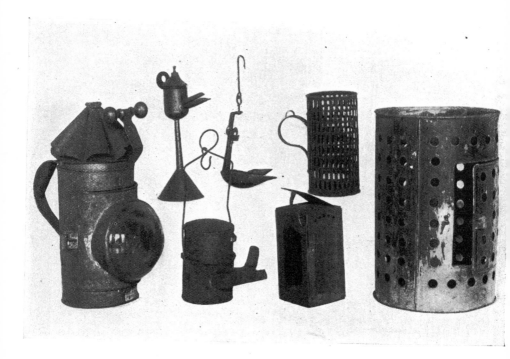

FIG. 30.—A GROUP OF OLD LANTERNS AND LAMPS.

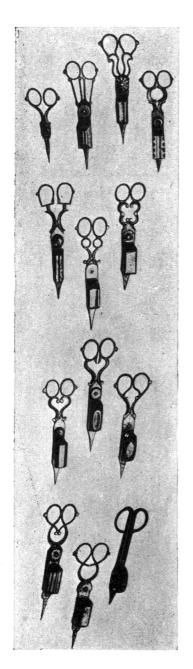

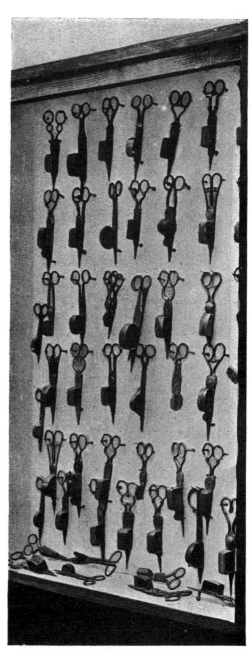

FIG. 31.—SNUFFERS.

FIG. 32.—SNUFFERS FROM THE EVERY
COLLECTION, LEWES.

30

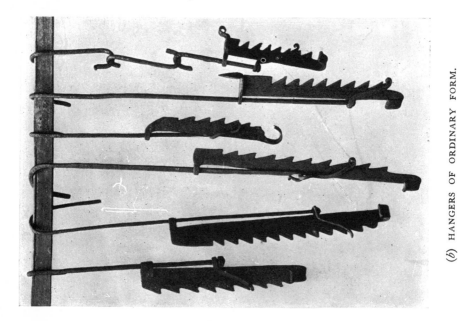

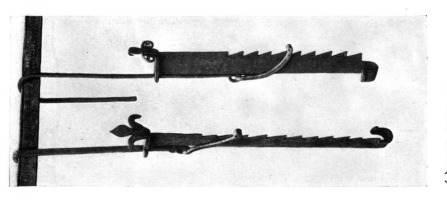

(*c*) HANGER ORNAMENTED WITH FIGURE OF SMITH AND TOOLS.

(*b*) HANGERS OF ORDINARY FORM.

(*a*) TWO VERY OLD HANGERS.

through and across the spiral was worked up as the candle burned shorter (Fig, 25). All these holders and candlesticks were either for table use or independent of the floor, but there were also tall standing ones, sometimes for two candles, and with an alternative fitting for rushes, that stood on the floor on wooden feet ; the candle holder sliding up and down the central iron rod and remaining at any point desired by the pressure of a spring (Fig. 23). Some of these standing candlesticks were all of wood, except the actual light holder. One of those shown in Fig. 27 allows the height to be regulated by means of a spike passing through the wooden column, the holes coming alternately in the turned spaces. The other (Fig. 26) has a wooden ratchet with wooden clip.

Brass candlesticks, for the most part of excellent design, were made in the eighteenth century ; some were of the usual yellow brass and others of a redder alloy, approaching the colour of copper. They were still made in the early nineteenth century, but in a debased form. All those shown in Fig, 29 were collected at farm and cottage sales, though many of them may have come from houses of a better class. Tallow candles and others of the earlier kinds required frequent snuffing, and a pair of snuffers with their accompanying tray went with the candles. Some of the very earliest were made of iron, but later they were always of brass (Figs. 31 and 32).

A contrivance for getting a light by flint and steel that was in use early in the nineteenth century was called a strike-a-light. It had a handle like a pistol and the same mechanism as a flint-lock musket. The flint held in the cock, when released by the trigger, struck against a raised steel plate attached to the round box that held the tinder, the impact both forcing up the lid and throwing a spark on to the tinder. Fig. 24 shows the two positions.

3

III.

THE HEARTH AND ITS IMPLEMENTS.

WHEN wood was the only fuel, except peat, in country districts, the wide " down " hearth was commonly used both for cooking and warming. It was equally suitable where, in some remote moorland places, there was no true peat for the alternative fuel— parings of peaty soils containing tufts of heath and gorse. In the simplest cottages the usual cooking utensil was the three-legged iron pot. It could either stand in the hot ashes on its three short legs or hang by the swinging handle. A few feet up the chimney was the wooden chimney bar, stretching across, the ends let into the masonry. It was of oak, or preferably, of chestnut ; in section higher than wide and with the upper edge rounded. Over this passed the curved top end of the hanger, an iron bar with a flat sheet-iron ratchet attachment looking like a coarse saw. The lowest end of the upright had either a closed loop or a knob, from which hung the hook that caught one of the teeth of the ratchet. The hanger could thus be set either high or low, according to the liveliness of the fire or the degree of heat required for the cooking. Some of the older hangers have an ornament at the top, usually a fleur-de-lys, or it might be a kind of lance head, or only a close curl of the end of the iron that connected the upper part of the ratchet with the upright bar (Fig. 36a). A rare example of a highly ornamented hanger is in the Victoria and Albert Museum. The loop that catches in the ratchet is decorated with elaborate scroll work and the lower part is pierced through, showing a silhouette of the smith at work, with some of his tools above (Fig. 36c). The most primitive form of hanger was the wooden " crochan," by which the pot, slung from above by a hazel rope, hung over the fire. The one illustrated, from the Hebrides, is now in the Edinburgh Museum (Fig. 37).

Fig. 37.
WOODEN
" CROCHAN "
FROM THE
HEBRIDES.

In farms and the better class of houses something more than the simple hanger was wanted. The fire was large and wide spread so that one point or another of its area might be the more convenient place for the cooking pot. Some contrivance for meeting this alternative was therefore needed and was provided by the chimney crane or pot crane; this was of two forms, one in which the horizontal bar was simply supported by a diagonal stay and the height of the pot adjusted by a short hanger at any point along the bar, and the other in which there are two movements of the crane itself; one to swing forward and back, and the other for raising or lowering the hook that holds the pot or kettle. In both forms the main vertical iron, the backbone of the whole concern, is so held at top and bottom that it can swing forward like a gate. The bottom end is commonly fitted into a piece

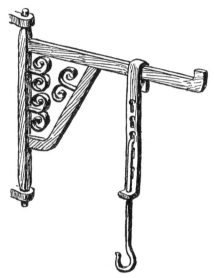

(a)—In a kitchen at Pontfaen, Pembrokeshire.

(b)—In kitchen of Old Rectory, Porthkerry, Glamorganshire.

Fig. 38.—CHIMNEY CRANES.

of hard stone and the top into a loop in an iron cramp built into the wall. At a certain distance along the horizontal arm a short iron strap suspends a lever or handle that has a hanging hook at the fire end, while the handle end rests under any one of the projecting buttons on the quadrant that is fixed near the upright, and thus the pot is held at any height above the fire. These cranes, made during the seventeenth and eighteenth centuries, show a great diversity of ornament. The main part of the structure was determined by the necessities of its use, and the smith then exercised his own powers of invention, taste and skill in various methods of enrichment. Sometimes it is only in the line or play of the different straps and stays, which, after doing their constructional work, were drawn out into curls or volutes with more or less closed ends, or it may be some ornamental twists of the square sectioned iron bar, or a little spray of leaf and flower, or even a whole tree with leafy branches and scroll tendrils, as in one fine example illustrated in Fig. 43. A number of these cranes, for the most part made in Sussex, but with one or two from the Midlands and the Eastern Counties, have been collected by Mr. J. H. Every, of the Phœnix Ironworks, Lewes ; they are now in his private museum, and some are here illustrated.

A simple form of iron firedog was in use in every cottage, generally of low shape so as not to interfere with the swinging pot ; the upright front being only high enough to stop a log of reasonable thickness from rolling out forwards ; and there were two loose iron bars that could be adjusted on the dogs so as to hold a cooking pot. But in some farmhouses, and even cottages, there were the tall-fronted cup dogs, with the tops framed in such a way as to hold a mug of hot drink. In these and in many other forms of tall-fronted dogs there was often an arrangement for supporting a spit. The illustration, Fig. 45, shows one with movable loops ; these would bring the spit to the front of the dogs. The loops or hooks were more frequently and more conveniently fixed to the back of the dogs, nearer to the fire. It was the pride of the good housewife to keep her spits bright, and they showed finely when displayed in the spitrack over the front of the fireplace. These spitracks were sometimes quite plain, but usually with the fronts of the projections handsomely moulded. Sometimes the spit was worked by a smoke-jack, a piece of mechanism whose power was derived from the draught in the chimney. In this case the spit had a circular disk at one end, the edge grooved to take the chain that connected it with the jack. In some old spits this circular wheel was larger, pointing to its having been used in the older days when turnspit dogs were the motive power. From the spit, a chain or cord was conveyed to the dog wheel fixed at some convenient height against the wall of the kitchen. The dog worked inside the wheel, whose flooring had transverse battens for his foothold. They were small, short legged, long bodied dogs, something the shape of a dachshund (Fig. 52).

Nowadays we roast more conveniently by hanging the joint vertically to the clockwork jack ; this also is better suited to the narrow shape of our coal fires. But in the old days, when the fire was on the hearth and was large and wide shaped to take a large piece of meat, there was no other way of roasting than the horizontal. For a heavy piece of meat there were two usual forms of spit ; one with two prongs which

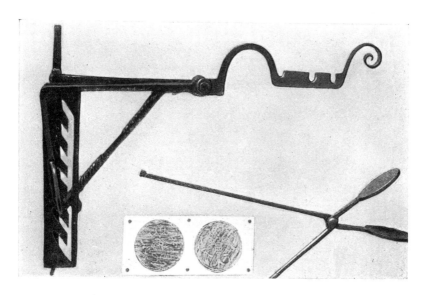

FIG. 39.—SMALL CHIMNEY CRANE AND GOFFER IRON.

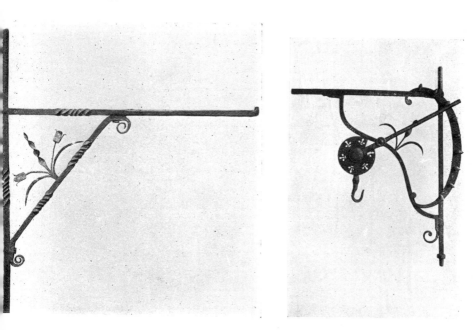

FIGS. 40, 41.—CHIMNEY CRANES WITH WROUGHT-IRON ORNAMENT.
(WARWICKSHIRE.)

FIG. 41.—A crane of good construction, the quadrant bracing both the horizontal
bar and the curved stay. The tulip ornament is rather weak. The round
plate pierced with six fleurs-de-lis is a quite unusual feature.

36

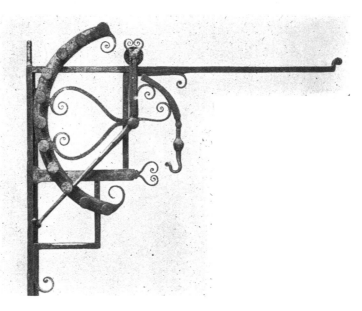

FIG. 42.—THREE-MOTION CHIMNEY CRANE.

FIG. 43.—HIGHLY ORNAMENTED CHIMNEY CRANE.

37

FIG. 44.—ELABORATE CHIMNEY CRANE.

FIG. 47.—ORNAMENTED CHIMNEY CRANE.

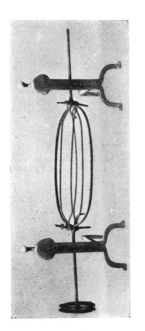

FIG. 45.—BASKET OR CRADLE SPIT.

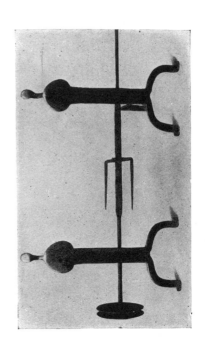

FIG. 46.—PRONGED ROASTING SPIT.

FIG. 48.—A PAIR OF CUP-DOGS.

FIG. 49.—COTTAGE FIRE-DOGS.

FIG. 51.—A SPITRACK.

FIG. 50.—ANCIENT FIRE-DOGS.

held it firm and the other, called a basket or cradle spit, in which the meat was enclosed, and held by a number of thin iron bars (Fig. 45). This was specially convenient for cooking a tender viand like a sucking pig, in whose case it was desirable to avoid piercing the meat and so letting out the succulent juices.

Many a pair of handsome old firedogs that had been in manorial houses found their way into farmhouses and cottages when iron firegrates came into use in the kitchens of houses of the better class. Some of them, of pure Gothic design, are of great antiquity. They might often be found fifty years ago in Surrey and Sussex, when attendance at farm sales in remote country places gave an opportunity of collecting many interesting relics of the older days.

Firebacks made in the old Sussex ironworks also came to light when they were pulled out to give place to the modern kitchen range, though in some cases those who made the alteration did not trouble to remove them and they have been found again in their original position when the fireplaces were restored to their earlier form. Many of them are of beautiful design with heraldic devices or finely treated grounds of tree form or foliated scroll work. One illustrated (Fig. 53) is of personal interest, showing the master ironfounder with his tools.

The tongs and fire shovels of the older times were of a fine simple shape, in happy contrast to the implements of the same name now to be found in shops, for the most part of bad design or overloaded with useless, so-called ornament. The reason is not far to seek, for the old tongs were made for actual use by the nearest smith, while the modern thing is one of thousands of the same, out of the ironmonger's pattern book. Really beautiful were some of the old brand tongs, small things to be held in one hand for picking up a brand and blowing it into flame for lighting a pipe or a rushlight. A selection from the Every collection is given in the Introduction. One of those illustrated in Fig. 63A was made towards the end of the eighteenth century by a country smith whose descendants are still numerous in the same district. It is a complete work of art, exactly right for its purpose, every line of it beautiful, with modest ornament of moulded shoulder and edging line—perfect in symmetry and balance. The ends that pick up the live charcoal are fashioned into little hands—even the spring that keeps it closed follows graceful curves. So it was that the old country smith worked ; thinking first of the use of the thing to be made and then putting into it everything of that tender beauty that comes of the pure joy of good craftsmanship.

4

Several forms of toasting implements were in use with the down fire ; some quite low for the cottage for toasting bacon or bread (Fig. 59). They stood on three short legs—two of them forward, under the actual toaster, and one half-way back, under the handle. The head with its two hoops was on a loose rivet and could be twisted a little way to one side or the other. The implement that is shown with the toaster is for raking hot potatoes out of the ashes. There were larger and more elaborate toasters in better houses, with tripod legs supporting an upright to which the actual toasting fork was fixed. In both the examples shown in Fig. 56 the toasting part slides up and down the standard and also revolves upon it, while it is kept in any position that may be desired by the pressure of a spring. In the one on the right hand there is another movement, for the horizontal fork pulls backward and forward.

A favourite device for tipping a kettle without taking it off the fire was the idleback or lazyback (Figs. 61–2). It hung on the hanger and it will be seen from the illustration how the act of pulling down the handle will tip the kettle. The hook nearest the spout has a spring clip that keeps the front of the kettle handle down when it is tipped for pouring. The old smith who forged it could not resist the suggestion of snake-like form in the handle of the tipper, for he finished off the end in a little snake's head. If it is noticed that in the picture the kettle does not hang level, it is because it is the way it takes of itself after being tipped.

A piece of old waggon tire, stood on edge, was commonly used in cottages as a fender, and a very handy fender it makes ; standing four inches high and about twenty inches long and with a pleasant curve, it was a neat way of keeping the ashes of the front of the fire in place.

Bellows have been in use for all time, but from their construction of wood and leather and from the need of their constant employment they had necessarily a rather short lifetime, and examples of those in common use dating further back than a hundred and fifty years are rare, though there are much older specimens in museums of a highly ornamental kind, in which both wooden faces were richly carved. The oldest we know of for ordinary household use had much longer handles and shorter bodies than the later patterns. A good kind of the late eighteenth and early nineteenth centuries had the turned body of a dark hardwood, as shown in one of the examples illustrated (Fig. 55). This had a nicely formed brass nozzle, and was altogether a shapely article. The ordinary kitchen bellows with elm body that is still to be had follows this, though on

FIG. 52.—A DOG TURNSPIT IN A KITCHEN AT NEWCASTLE EMLYN, SOUTH WALES.

By Thomas Rowlandson; about 1800.

FIG. 53.—FIREBACK WITH PORTRAIT OF THE IRONFOUNDER,
"MASTER LEONARD," AND HIS TOOLS, 1636.

FIG. 54.—HERALDIC FIREBACK, GROOMBRIDGE PLACE, KENT, 1604.

FIG. 55.—BELLOWS.

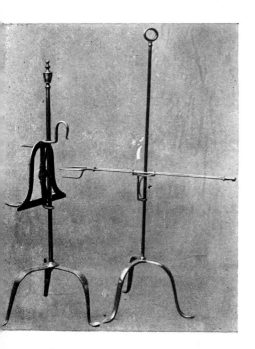

FIG. 56.—TWO STANDING TOASTERS.

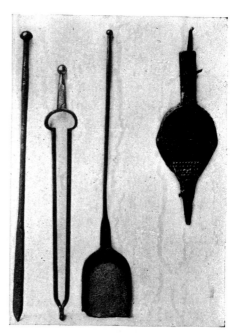

FIG. 57.—FIRE IRONS AND VERY OLD
BELLOWS.

FIG. 58.—LONG-HANDLED COPPER
FRYING PAN.

FIG. 59.—TOASTER AND POTATO RACK.

FIG. 60.—SALT BOX.

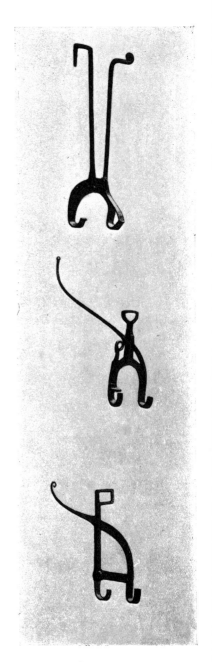

FIG. 61.—IDLEBACKS.

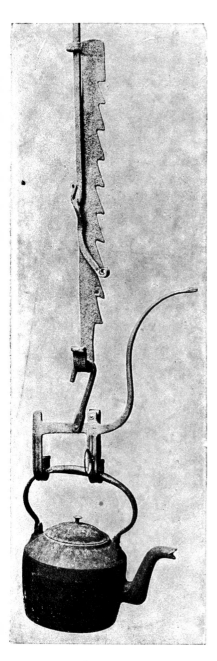

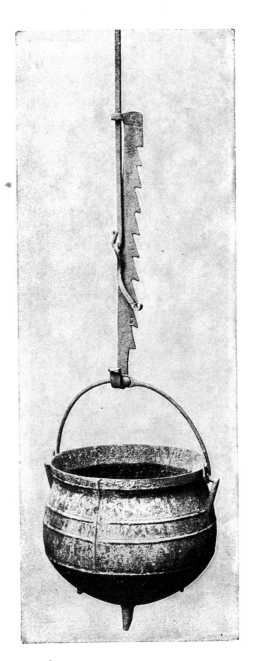

FIG. 62.—IDLEBACK.   FIG. 63.—LARGE IRON POT ON HANGER.

FIG. 63A.
BRAND TONGS.

FIG. 64.—MECHANICAL BELLOWS.

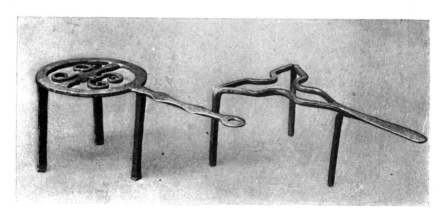

FIG. 65.—IRON TRIVETS.

FIG. 66.—VARIOUS SKILLETS.

FIG. 67.—PIPKINS IN STONEWARE AND GLAZED EARTHENWARE.

FIG.71.—IRON SKEWERS.

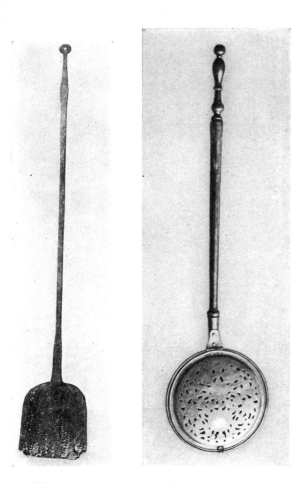

FIG. 68.—OVEN PEEL.   FIG. 69.—WARMING PAN.

FIG. 70.—SUGAR NIPPERS.   FIG. 72.—KNIFE BOX.

coarser lines. An ingenious form of bellows, giving a continuous blast, was in use in the early years of the nineteenth century (Fig. 64). It has a drum-shaped body narrowing into a square channel that ends in a brass nozzle. Inside the drum is a wheel with floats. Outside there is an arrangement of two wheels with driving bands, the larger with a handle, which turn the wheel within, the multiplied power making a steady draught. There is an old saying among cottage folk in Sussex descriptive of some situation that is full of difficulty or almost hopeless : " It is a case of green wood and no bellows."

The main cooking utensil was the iron pot, still made and now largely exported to some half-barbarous peoples. It would either swing from the hook of a hanger or stand down in the ashes. There were also skillets of brass or bronze which appear to have been cast in one piece. They were thick and heavy and look as if they would wear and endure for ever. In fact, a great many more of these would have been still in existence but that in Jacobean times a quantity were called in and melted down for bronze coinage. A later form of skillet was of wrought brass, much thinner. This kind had a projecting rim, the brass being brought over a wired edge, and they dropped into iron holders on three legs. Large brass cauldrons were used for heating milk in cheese-making. Iron trivets, on which any cooking pot could be stood, or anything placed to keep warm, were in many good patterns. Frying pans had the handles very long, sometimes as much as three and half feet ; the necessity of this will be seen when the size of the wood fire and the distance for the comfort of the operator are considered.

There were also earthen cooking pots ; pipkins with handles, in stoneware with a dull glaze, both inside and out, and in different kinds of earthenware ; some all glazed, and others, of the commonest kind, of the ordinary redware, glazed inside only. They were used either seated in the hot ashes or raised on trivets. Cakes and small loaves were baked in the ashes under a redware pot turned upside down. The girdle, still much used in the north and occasionally all over England, is of great antiquity ; it can either hang to a hanger or stand on a trivet.

IV.

IN THE COTTAGE KITCHEN.

STILL in the neighbourhood of the fire in the old cottage and farm-house kitchen was the salt-box—handy for cooking and within range of the warmth for keeping the contents dry. Also the knife box, which hung upright on a nail ; the panelled lid slid upwards for opening. The knife handles were of bullock horn or of buckhorn, the best of all knife handle materials. Various lesser implements, skimmers, ladles, and a large fork for getting a heavy piece of boiled meat out of the pot hung handily near the fireplace, and a set of iron skewers were on their double-hooked hanger. Some of the older skewers had the heads finished with a tight curl of flattened iron or even two such curls, that formed a suitable ornament.

Sugar nippers were found only in houses of the better class. Till the middle of the nineteenth century white sugar was bought in whole loaves. They were first broken into large pieces and then cut with the nippers into a convenient size for use. The kitchen chimney piece, which at the present day, alas ! usually shows only an assortment of sordid shop tins, had its appropriate dressing of pretty china ornaments ; figures, singly or in groups ; cottages and sheep-dogs were the favourite subjects. They could be bought in china shops till about the year 1860, but a stall of them was always to be found at fairs which were then usual throughout the country. The cowjug and money box (Fig. 74), were also such articles as could be bought at fairs. The fine old Toby jug was the pride of the farmhouse kitchen chimney shelf. It shows a stout eighteenth century farmer in a three-cornered hat which forms the open top of the jug. He wears a shirt with ruffled bands and a long flowered coat and holds his mug of ale upon his knee. In the example shown the right foot is broken, but his pipe lies beside it, and his beer barrel, very small in proportion, is between his feet. There might still be in the farmhouse one of the heavy stoneware mugs dating from the earlier years of the eighteenth century. Much of the old traditional ornament of later eighteenth-century work has been preserved and perpetuated

IG. 73.—SHEPHERD AND SHEPHERDESS

FIG. 74.—COW JUG.

IG. 75.—EARTHENWARE MONEY BOX, 1837.

FIG. 76.—TOBY JUG.

FIG. 77.—EIGHTEENTH CENTURY STONEWARE MUGS.

FIG. 78.—MODERN LAMBETH STONEWARE.

FIG. 79.—BED WAGON.

FIG. 80.—BRASS DREDGERS, PEPPER POTS, SPOON, AND BOX

by Messrs. Doulton in their stoneware potteries at Lambeth. Probably they have some of the original moulds ; if not, they have been faithfully copied and their character accurately retained. Mugs, tobacco jars and beerjugs—the best beerjugs possible—are decorated with figures in relief of a farmer sitting on a barrel with his mug of ale on a small three-legged table ; or the same kind of figure smoking his long clay pipe with his dog by his side; or a tree, a windmill, or a stag hunt, or all of them combined on one of the larger pieces, as shown in Fig. 77. Then on the chimney shelf there was sure to be a pair of brass candlesticks, much cherished and kept brightly polished, and very likely a brass or pewter pepper-pot and one or two horn mugs.

Not far from the fireplace hung the warming pan ; a decorative object in itself ; the lid of the pan pierced in some ornamental design, often enriched with engraving, and the hardwood handle finished with some pretty turned work, as seen in Fig. 69. These eighteenth-century warming pans were made equally in brass or copper. The lid is hinged and opens back to the handle. They were for use with charcoal or hot embers from the wood fire. The more modern closed copper warming pan for hot water was a safer thing and remained till the middle of the nineteenth century when it went out of use in favour of a tin or copper warmer that could be left in the bed, or the still more accommodating india-rubber hot-water bottle.

Though its place is not in the farmhouse kitchen, another old contrivance for warming a bed may here be described. It is the old bed-waggon (illustrated by Fig. 79), in use from the earlier years of the eighteenth century, and possibly from a still more remote date. It was a cumbersome thing from three to four feet long, made all of oak ; the main structure consisting of four rails connected by four flattened hoops, and with rods that acted both as ties and stretchers. In the middle, resting on the bottom part of the framework was an iron tray on which was a trivet for holding the pan of hot ashes. Over this, attached to the underside of the upper part of the frame was a piece of sheet iron corresponding to the tray below. This and the tray prevented any scorching of the bedclothes.

The most usual drinking vessel of cottage or farmhouse, other than those of pewter or stoneware, was the horn mug. It was made of a section of bullock's horn, and from the natural shape it tapered just rightly. The bottom was a disk of horn that fitted into a groove and made so tight a joint that it was absolutely waterproof. To this day, a thin-edged horn is one of the pleasantest things from which to drink beer

5

or cider.   By the middle of the nineteenth century, pewter mugs, which till then had been in use in farms were, for the most part, to be seen in public houses, where they acted both as measures and drinking vessels ; they were commonly engraved with the owner's name. Examples appear in Fig. 83.

Earthenware pitchers had been in use for centuries. It is a pity that their general use has gone out though they are still to be had in the western counties.   Early in the nineteenth century the use of crockery became general, and in fifty years' time, even in public houses, earthenware mugs and jugs took the place of the old time pewter. The northern potteries sent their ware in quantity by barge to the middle and southern counties, and Bristol in the south-west distributed its capital jugs and mugs with their old traditional ornament, much of the same character as that of the Lambeth potteries on the same class of ware.   Both types are shown on page 58 (Figs. 84-5).

Every farm and cottage had its wooden harvest bottles ; little barrels made of tough oak hooped with iron, with a projecting mouthpiece convenient to drink from.   The cord by which it was carried or hung up at home passed through the two ends of the mouthpiece and was secured either by a knot or, in the case of more careful workmanship, by a wooden peg driven in tight so that nothing need project.   The cord was nearly always of plaited horsehair, white and black, or of three colours.   The owner's initials were incised or branded on the heads ; often the two heads would be almost covered with lettering, some of ancient character, showing a number of successive ownerships.   These harvest bottles are still in use, and may well be, for nothing, as to convenience both for carrying and drinking, can well take their place ; drinking out of an ordinary bottle is an awkward and unsightly performance.   A glazed earthenware bottle called a Dorset pill, for harvest use, was, and may still be, made in that county ; the name is probably a survival from the tradition of the pilgrim's bottle.

The leather bottles, near in shape to the wooden harvest bottle, were made in the seventeenth and eighteenth centuries and probably earlier ; one may even think of them as descendants of the wine-skins of antiquity.   The oldest of those now in museums and private collections are of Jacobean or possibly Tudor days.   The leather bottle had a stumpy mouthpiece and raised shoulders nearly level with it through which the thong for carrying was passed.   It was made in one piece, all but the heads that were sewn in.   When they went out of use they had a piece cut out of the upper part of one side and were hung up in

FIG. 81.—HORN MUGS.

FIG 82.—RED EARTHENWARE PITCHERS.

FIG. 83.—PEWTER MUGS.

FIG. 84.—COLOURED MUGS FROM NORTHERN POTTERIES.

FIG. 85.—BRISTOL WARE.

FIG. 86.—HARVEST BOTTLES.

FIG. 87.—GLASS BOTTLES OF A CENTURY AGO.

FIG 88.—PATTENS.

FIG 89.—LEATHER BOTTLES.

FIG. 90.—THE BELL RINGER'S BLACK JACK OF LINCOLN.

cart sheds for holding wheel-grease. This new use probably added to their lifetime, for grease feeds leather so effectively that if regularly applied the leather will last almost indefinitely. There were also the great leather jugs, known as Black Jacks, that remained as practical jugs till near the end of the eighteenth century. Some of the largest and best preserved belonged to local corporations or associations and were of a ceremonial character. Some were even fitted with handsome silver lids. One large Black Jack is silver-mounted and has a medallion of Oliver Cromwell inserted on the lid. It is of seventeenth century work. There are inscriptions round the silver rim and on the lid, and a coat-of-arms is engraved in the leather on the front. The leather was all in one piece except the circular bottom. The body of the jug was shaped by being fitted, when the leather was soaked and soft, over a wooden block. Two Jacks of the late eighteenth century are shown in the illustration in Fig. 90; they held the ringer's beer; the one of which two sides are shown was painted with a bell and a shield of the municipal arms, besides the inscription.

Glass bottles of the eighteenth century had short bodies and long necks; they would stack together though rather uneven in shape, but by the end of the century they were discarded in favour of the present bottle of long-bodied shape.

The old farmhouse and the better class of labourers' cottage had a capacious back kitchen. Here was the sink for washing up, with its accompanying draining board and rack. Here also was the brick oven for baking bread; it showed on the outside as a semi-circular projection with a rounded top and had its own little roof. The inside was all brick; the floor flat, the sides upright for a few courses, and then arched barrel-shape. A faggot of dry brushwood went in, was lighted, and by the time it was all burnt and the ashes raked out it would be the right heat for baking. Inside the back kitchen the top of the oven was stepped back in brickwork, corresponding with the rounded back outside. The mouth of the oven showed as a flat arch with a door of sheet iron with two handles that moved right out (Figs. 91, 92). The loaves were put in and drawn out with a sort of flat, long-handled shovel called the oven peel; it was usually of iron, but sometimes of wood (Fig. 68). The wood peel is interesting, showing its derivation from the French *pelle*, the name of the long-handled shovel commonly in use in France and Italy, and still surviving in our own country in the extreme south-west, as the Cornish shovel.

In the coolest place in the back kitchen was the barrel of home-

brewed beer or cider and any home-made wine either in a barrel or large
stoneware bottle. Overhead was the bacon rack, so placed that it
received a draught of air between the outer door and a window. Hams
sewn up in canvas to keep off flies hung from overhead beams and
bunches of herbs for flavouring or physic. The main beams and the
stout oak joists between had nails in their sides for hanging up all sorts
of useful things—baskets, sieves, a spare beehive, and so on ; all within
easy sight and convenient hand reach. A stout, low shelf held bags of
meal and flour. Here also were the mistress's pattens, extinct since
the invention of india-rubber goloshes and the better making and
draining of roads and footways, but still in use within the memory of
old people. The patten is a clog with a wooden sole ; it has a leather
toe-piece and leather bands that tie together over the instep. An oval iron
hoop on two short legs is fixed underneath, raising the wearer well out
of any but the deepest mud (Fig. 88). As a child I remember being
always amused by seeing the sharp prints of the pattens on the village
footpath, and my father told me that the sentries posted at the park
gates in London had orders to turn back any women wearing pattens,
to avoid injury to the gravel paths.

In the end of the eighteenth century the use of tea was beginning to
take the place at some meals, of beer, which had hitherto been used at all.
The illustration, Fig. 93, is from a beautiful picture in the Victoria and
Albert Museum, dated 1793, of a woman with the kettle on the down
fire and bellows in hand making ready for her tea. She is a solitary
cottage dweller, for there is one cup only on the three-legged tea table.
The kitchen living-room shows the usual articles of utility of a fairly
well-to-do cottager. A shelf holds some square wooden trenchers, round-
hollowed in the middle, with a small circular pit for salt in one of the
spandrils. A Dutch clock is on the wall, with a warming pan and sundry
kitchen implements. Her cloak hangs over the back of her rush-seated
chair. She wears a light coloured gown with a *panier* at the back, and
a large black bonnet that frames her beautiful serious old face. No wonder
that the artist, W. B. Bigg, R.A., took the pleasure that is evident in
painting this scene of quiet country life. William Cobbett, writing
twenty-eight years later, denounced tea with his usual vehemence, even
going so far as to call it a " degrading curse." Comparing it with beer,
he says :—" It is notorious that it contains nothing nutritious, that it,
besides being good for nothing, has badness in it. . . . . It is,
in fact, a weaker kind of laudanum, which enlivens for the moment and
deadens afterwards." In page after page of his chapters on brewing

FIG. 92.—INTERIOR VIEW.

FIG. 91.—EXTERIOR VIEW.   THE BRICK OVEN, SURREY.

64

FIG. 93.—AN OLD WOMAN PREPARING TEA.

From a Painting by W. B. Bigg, R.A., 1793.

beer in that entertaining book " Cottage Enonomy " he falls foul of the " clattering tea tackle," regretting with all the strength of his powerful vocabulary that whereas in his younger days every cottager brewed his own wholesome beer, the good custom was dying out and giving place at some meals to the drinking of the pernicious tea.

V.

OLD COTTAGE AND FARMHOUSE FURNITURE.

THOSE who were born before the middle of the nineteenth century may remember the good furniture of cottage and farmhouse, now, alas ! but rarely seen in those places for which it was so admirably fitted. In the farmhouse, in the old days when the labourers ate in the farm kitchen, there was the great oak table, seven to eight feet long, with a fixed bench against the wall of the same length, and a separate oak form on the free side. The one shown in the Introduction (Fig. 2) came from a farmhouse, and except that it has lost one lower back rail, probably worn through by long friction with hobnailed shoes and boots, is as sound and strong as ever. The framing under the table top shows the date 1599, the next year after the defeat of the Spanish Armada, when Queen Elizabeth's reign had yet four years to run. Besides the long table the main feature of the kitchen was the dresser ; the lower part a narrow table with deep drawers and two turned legs in front. It was usual for the back not to have legs, but to rest on a stout fillet fixed to the wall. The upper part was a series of two or three shelves ; in the best examples the shelves grew wider as they rose. On these was a handsome display of crockery ; the fine old willow pattern was the prime favourite from the time it came into general use till well into the middle of the nineteenth century. In most cases the dresser went up to the underside of the joists which in the old cottages were not more than seven feet from the floor. It had a top and often a sort of scalloped wooden valance. Some had boarded backs, but those in cottages usually had no back, the wall showing between the shelves (Fig. 95).

In many of the old houses there would still be the joint stool, the carver's seat at the end of the table. Sometimes such a seat was converted into a small low table by having a round table top that slid on to the top of the stool (Fig. 109). Chairs were of the good old Windsor pattern, either with plain railed back or the handsomer wheel back. There were several older patterns of chairs much alike in design, oak-framed and rush-bottomed or seated with wicker ; later the same kind of chairs were made of beech and stained black. A good child's chair was in use in the better houses (Figs. 94, 96, 97, 98, 99).

The oak settle was frequent in the older farmhouse ; a ponderous piece of furniture almost as solid as a panelled room partition ; of much comfort in winter time when partly enclosing the great open wood fire and stopping draughts from the back. The eight-day clock in its tall oak case completed the more important pieces of furniture of the farmhouse living kitchen or that of the better class of labourer's cottage, or it might be a less costly 24-hour clock, but still with a good oak case. The cheaper Dutch clock with its pretty painted face was to be seen in some cottages (Fig. 101). An odd piece of furniture might sometimes be seen where there was a growing family of young children. It was called a baby-runner (Fig. 104). The upright rod fitted at the foot into a hole in the floor and into a beam or joist overhead and the ring went round the child's body at a suitable height, allowing it to move anywhere within the radius of the contrivance, but safe from the fire or other danger.

Upstairs there would be at least one solid bed, either of oak or of commoner wood painted, with head and footboards panelled and, perhaps, moulded. In a good farmhouse there was sure to be a handsome four-poster with curtains and top valance. The wooden cradle of seventeenth century design (Fig. 105), was from a cottage ; its solid head tells of the need of protection from draught ; it has rockers and handles at both ends. Many a good old oak chest of drawers was in the farmhouses, and others found their way into cottages when oak furniture went out of fashion in better houses in favour of mahogany ; the same influence accounts for the finding in cottages of the old oak bible boxes that are now treasured by collectors. Of the same date as the earlier chests of drawers were the best of the large chests known as linen hutches (Figs. 106, 107). Some such chests had already been in use for clothing also before the more convenient form with running drawers became general. The oldest of these are of small size made of plain oak boards, but the larger ones for storing linen are handsome things, well framed, with moulded fronts and ends and in many cases with richly carved panels. It was usual to have a shallow drawer at the bottom, but inside all was clear except for a small receptacle just at the top, about four inches deep and not much wider. It was at one end, of the whole width from back to front, and was for holding mending material and any small gear that might easily go astray in the large inside space.

Besides its good design, the old oak furniture owes something of its ornamental effect to the brass scutcheons of the drop handles and key-holes (Figs. 108 and 110). Those for the keyholes admitted of a wide diversity of pattern ; the ones for the drop handles had to follow a more general plan as indicated by the handle, but were much varied in detail. The later ones of the eighteenth century were of cast brass and are shown in some of the earliest of the tradesmens' pattern books.

PEWTER.

The use of pewter for table ware followed that of the wooden trencher, though the trencher remained in use in the labourer's cottage till near the year 1830. An old country carpenter said to me, in the year 1904 :— " I mind when we always ate off wooden trenchers, not crockern plates." Pewter was worked in France as early as in the fourteenth century, but it was mostly for objects of ornament, such as coats-of-arms for wall decoration, or small objects such as the scallop shells worn in pilgrims' hats. For some hundreds of years also, pewter was the one metal, other than gold and silver, that might be used for sacramental plate. By the middle of the fourteenth century a guild of pewterers was established in England, with a strict code of ordinances, in order to maintain a high grade of material and workmanship. It was first known as the Craft of Pewterers, but later as the Company of Pewterers.

It is very commonly supposed that all pewter has in its composition a basis, if not a rather large proportion, of lead, but the best kind had no lead at all. It was an alloy of copper or brass with tin and was known as fine pewter. There are records of some cooking vessels of Edward I being of pewter ; this could not have been reconciled with our idea of it as a soft metal that could not possibly stand the fire. A set of table ware, dishes, plates, and small basins for holding sauces and condiments, called saucers—a dozen of each—was called a " garnish," no doubt because when not in actual use it was kept displayed on a buffet in the dining hall. To this were commonly added candlesticks, also flagons, tankards, salt-cellars and any other pieces (Figs. 111–113).

But in these early days pewter was only in use in palaces and in the houses of the greater nobility and ecclesiastical establishments ; but during the fifteenth century its use became more general among people of the well-to-do classes, and a hundred years later a set of pewter ware was in the possession of every prosperous farmer. During all this time

FIG. 95.—OAK DRESSER WITH WILLOW WARE.

FIG. 94.—CHILD'S CHAIR FROM CRANBROOK, KENT

FIG 96.—OLD RAIL-BACK AND ORDINARY WINDSOR CHAIR

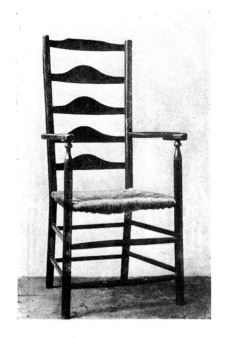

FIG. 97.—RUSH-BOTTOMED CHAIR.

FIG. 98.—WHEEL-BACK WINDSOR
ARMCHAIR.

71

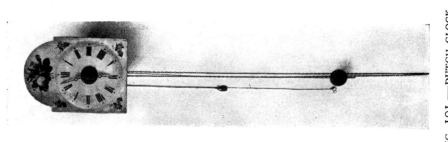

FIG. 100.—TWENTY-FOUR HOUR CLOCK.　　FIG. 101.—DUTCH CLOCK.

FIG 99 —EIGHT-DAY CLOCK

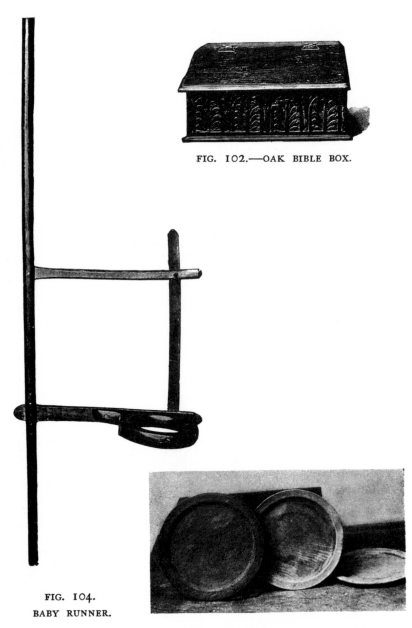

FIG. 102.—OAK BIBLE BOX.

FIG. 104.
BABY RUNNER.

FIG. 103.—WOODEN TRANCHERS.

FIG. 105 —SEVENTEENTH CENTURY CRADLE.

FIG. 106.—OAK CLOTHES HUTCH.

FIG. 107.—CARVED OAK LINEN HUTCH.

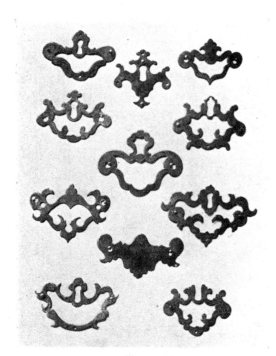

FIG. 108.—HANDLE AND KEYHOLE SCUTCHEONS.

FIG. 109.—JOINT STOOL WITH TABLE TOP.

FIG. 110.—EARLY BRASS
KEYHOLE SCUTCHEONS.

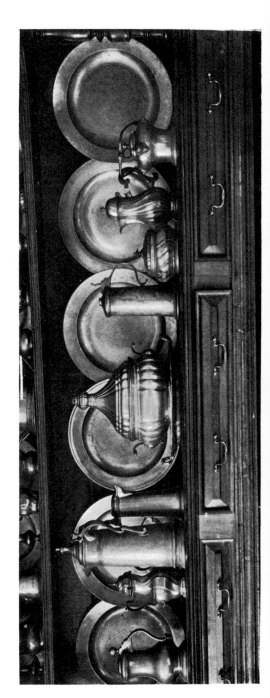

FIG. 111.—PEWTER INKSTANDS AND CANDLESTICK.

FIG. 113.—PEWTER PEPPER POTS AND SALTS.

Exterior.

Interior, showing Old Fittings.

FIGS 114 and 115.—THE PRIESTS HOUSE, WEST HOATHLY, SUSSEX.
(*Vide also Fig. 4.*)

the large dishes, called chargers, had the flat wide edge that gives so much dignity to the older ware ; the later dishes, with wired or moulded edges, are far less impressive.

Following a kind of family tradition, a set of pewter plates and dishes were used in the servants' hall in some large houses till well into the nineteenth century, long after the use of earthenware had become general, but by the middle of the century they were almost entirely given up. Stray pieces found their way into cottages, where later they were collected by dealers, and by the end of the century they had become solely objects of antiquity.

Pewter dishes, and especially plates, of the older pattern are not so numerous as they might have been, for as they became worn and battered they were melted down and moulded afresh ; so that though the actual metal may have been the same for centuries, yet the manufactured article would be of a comparatively recent date.

The interior of the Priest's House at West Hoathly, in Sussex (Figs. 4 and 115), which has been preserved as a kind of local museum, shows the furnishing that was usual in a farmhouse or other small private dwelling in the eighteenth and in the early part of the nineteenth century.

7

VI.

COTTAGE CONSTRUCTION.

A T the present time we have greatly to regret the loss of local tradition in building. In the older days when communication was difficult and the transport of weighty material from a distance was impossible, building was done with what was nearest at hand. By long use of the means available, the way of treatment became crystallised into a distinct manner or local style. In many districts where there was much woodland, timber was the building staple, and the whole framing of the house was of wood. In the north and middle of England, in some of the earliest existing cottages, and in many that have been pulled down within living memory, the main construction was with what are known as " crucks " (Fig. 116). These are long, heavy timbers, roughly squared and split in pairs out of trees that have a natural curve ; the butts are set on a rough stone base and the tops meet at the heavy squared ridge ; there was a pair at each end, or for a larger building a third pair in the middle of the length. Heavy tie-beams pass across, notched and pinned to the crucks ; their ends project beyond the crucks and carry the wall plate. Purlins are also notched and pinned to the main framing, giving a bearing to the rafters before they spread out to the wall plate. Thus the whole structure of the roof is formed before the walls are built. This method of construction prevailed throughout Yorkshire and all the north and middle of England to the borders of Wales, but was unknown in the south and east.

It is noticeable that even in districts where stone abounds cottages seem to have been rarely built with stone walls in ancient times. As late as the seventeenth century even better class houses were built with clay and wattle. It has not been generally observed, but a reason for this may be found, in assuming that the cottage builders were simple peasants who constructed their own dwellings, without the aid of the skilled mason, who alone could work in stone. The old Teutonic word for a peasant, " Bauer," meaning builder, would favour such a presumption. It was not till well into the seventeenth century, when much forest land had been cleared and timber commanded a higher price, that it was found to be as cheap to build houses of stone. But the traditions of timber building remained, and well into the eighteenth century cottages were still built with wooden framing. The filling, in these later examples was commonly of brick, but in the earlier, not only the fillings, but partitions and even whole walls were of wattle and daub. In the timber framing, upright rods of hazel were sprung into prepared grooves, and smaller rods were woven in and out horizontally after the manner of basket work, or as, to the present day, the country workman makes the wattle hurdles for use in sheepfolds. For the daub, clay mixed to a thick mud with water and with straw added, all well trodden or pounded together, was plastered in ; in the best work, by two men working against each other from opposite sides. A mixture of cow dung with the clay and straw made a good daub and dried hard, and a useful variant had a proportion of chalk or lime. While still wet the daub was scratched over with a pointed stick or a coarse broom to give a " key " to a final finer plastering. Hazel was found to be the most durable for the wattling ; in buildings lately demolished, dating from Jacobean and even Elizabethan times, the upright rods have been found quite sound ; even the little silvery spots and streaks that are the natural markings of the bark being clearly visible (Fig. 117).

Cottages in many parts of Devon were built of cob and thatched. Such cottages are remarkable for comfort—warm in winter and cool in summer ; they are absolutely weatherproof if the thatch is kept in good repair, and they are built on a solid foundation brought up a foot or more out of the ground. When properly made a cob wall is so durable that there are farmhouses and cottages of this material still standing that were built in the reign of Queen Elizabeth. Almost any kind of clayey or stiffish soil serves for cob. A house recently erected to the design of the late Mr. E. W. Gimson is built in this old manner and thatched (Fig. 118), and the subject is now so much engaging the attention of owners and architects that a revival of cob building may be looked for. It is not only a cheap way of building, but the comfort of its two-feet thick walls is beyond comparison with that of cottages of any other ordinary material. It is made in much the same way as earthen walling in other parts of England. The soil is mixed with water and wheat straw, well trodden together, and turned and trodden again till it is thoroughly incorporated. It is laid on the wide plinth of stone, brick or concrete, each fork full not flat, but with a diagonal slope, and again trodden firmly. Every such layer is left to dry before another is put on, so that it is not a quick process ; for the same reason it is a convenience and economy of labour to have several jobs within easy reach going on at the same time. The first laid cob must not be exposed to rain, but must be covered with some temporary protection.

Another system of earth walling was practised in the eastern counties, where cottage walls were built with sun-dried clay lumps—and another method, nearly allied to the use of Devonshire cob, was employed in chalk districts. Here the chalk was quarried towards the end of the year and laid out in lumps to be broken up by frost. In the spring it was mixed with straw and water and when well trodden and of the right consistency it was forked up on to the prepared courses of solid plinth and trodden firm; small knobs of chalk were mixed with the mud formed by the water and the more finely divided chalk. It had an external plastering such as would now be represented by cement, or a mixture of cement and lime mortar.

There is an old cottage of remarkable beauty at Bignor in Sussex, dating from Tudor times, and lately injudiciously restored. Two views are given (Figs. 119, 120). The massive timber structure rests on a solid plinth of rubble stone walling. The upper storey, at the two ends comes forward, carried on the two main beams and the heavy joists of nearly square section. A moulded string under the upper windows is of ornamental value. The brick and flint filling of some of the panels between the timbering is evidently of later date; the original filling was no doubt of wattle and daub. The doorway, which comes under the right hand projection, has moulded jambs and a moulded, flat-arched top. The projection of the ends gives a recessed effect to the middle of the front which is accentuated by the heavy shade. The roof is of thatch. It must have been built originally for something better than an ordinary cottage for, till late in the reign of Queen Elizabeth, these were of much slighter and flimsier construction. But in Stuart times many good cottages and small houses were built, though still with timber framing and wattled walls; many of them were plastered over the whole wall surface. A great number of these remain to this day, and their good proportion and excellent way of employing local material are an example that modern architects are not slow to appreciate. Many such good cottages would have been built anew of late years but for the hindrances occasioned by the building by-laws. Their provisions, in many cases quite unreasonable, and the bad proportion insisted on, have deterred many owners from building the much needed cottages which would have been erected if they had had a free hand. It is quite right that there should be protection from the bad, cheap cottages of

FIG. 116.—NORTHERN "CRUCK" CONSTRUCTION.

FIG 117.—"WATTLE AND DAUB," WEST BURTON, WEST SUSSEX.

FIG. 118.—A MODERN COB-WALLED THATCHED COTTAGE, DESIGNED BY THE LATE

FIGS 119, 120.—AN OLD TIMBER COTTAGE, BIGNOR, SUSSEX.

FIG. 121.—GARNETTED JOINTS.

FIG. 122.—" THE ELLIOTTS," MOUSEHILL, SURREY.

the jerry builder, but where owners only wish to build well, with the design of a competent architect, and with all regard to sound construction, comfort and good sanitation, it is much to be regretted that they are not allowed to do it.

The picture, Fig. 117, of a portion of the walling of an old farm building in West Sussex shows the rougher kind of wattle filling within a timber framing, the earthy daub having fallen off in some places. Cottages of rather later date throughout the home counties commonly had the spaces that were formerly wattled filled in with brick or some local stone; the nature of the filling depending on the material most conveniently obtainable. In districts where bricks were made there would also be roofing tiles. The large unbroken tiled roof, mossed and coloured with lichens, gives the cottage an appearance of comfortable protection, and its surface is pleasantly varied by the shallow furrows from eaves to ridge, showing where the weight of the tiling had borne down the lesser rafters between the principals.

As forest land was cleared and timbered structure gave way to walling in brick and stone, a study of the old cottages shows many pretty ways of using the newer material. In an old cottage at Moushill, in South-west Surrey (Fig. 122), the doorway is arched in brick and the wall above the parlour window has a cleverly formed relieving arch in brickwork. Three brick courses are next above this, repeated on the same level over the doorway, and another three courses of the same drop down between. In brick also is the framing of the windows, and between the upper windows are brick panels with recessed circles that appear to have been plastered, probably for some inscription or ornament. The remainder of the wall is of the local Bargate stone. In many cottages in these southern counties of the same date, the wall of the ground floor rises in brick or stone and that of the upper floor is tile hung, on battens nailed on outside the studding, and lath and plaster within. As the studding rises flush with the wall below, the thickness of the battens and tiles forms a slight projection, accentuated by the lower courses of tiles being set out at the bottom, the better to throw off rain and so keep the walling and foundation dry. Some of the old walling in the same district, built of the local stone in pieces of uneven shape, had small chippings of the black iron stones that are found in the surface of the heathy tracts, pressed into the mortar, so forming what are known as " garnetted " joints (see illustration, Fig. 121). This was noticed by Gilbert White, in his " History of Selborne." In one of his letters, written about the year 1760, we read :—" From a notion of rendering their work the more elegant, and giving it a finish, the masons chip this stone into small fragments about the size of the head of a large nail, and then stick the pieces into the wet mortar along the joints of their freestone walls ; this embellishment carries an odd appearance, and has occasioned strangers sometimes to ask us pleasantly whether we fastened our walls together with tenpenny nails."

Almshouses built any time within the last three hundred years show many delightful buildings throughout the length and breadth of the land and are good records of the best type of local building as applied to cottage dwellings.   The row of these houses at Ross, in Herefordshire (Fig. 124), has much in common with what prevails in the Cotswolds which are, in fact, not so very far distant to the south-east. They are an example of the quiet dignity that comes of the use of large stone in the walling, of the important lintels and the mullioned windows. In the illustration the quiet effect is partly disturbed by the straight, hard line of iron guttering that takes the rain water from the short sections of eaves that come between the dormers ; a modern convenience that does not help the architecture.   The charming row of almshouses at Mapledurham on the same page gain something of the same dignity from the bold use of wrought stone about the doors and windows.

Hall's almshouses at Bradford-on-Avon (Fig. 125) are in another district of good stone walling.   The whole building is beautiful in its quiet simplicity, and has features of much refinement in the treatment of the gateway to the road, in the panel of sculptured arms of the founder over the middle doorway (Fig. 126), and in the handsome stone urns that stand upon the wall that encloses the narrow strip of garden ground.

Some of the most beautiful of our cottages and other buildings are to be found in the Cotswolds, the hilly range of Oolite limestone that runs for fifty miles through Gloucestershire ; even the cottage windows are stone mullioned, giving great dignity to the humble dwellings.

In chalky districts, as in Hampshire and elsewhere, and especially in the case of church towers and buildings of some importance, may be seen the chequered walls of chalk and flint. Flint is not a good building material, the shape of the lumps being unkind to masonry and of so little length that there is no means of getting a good tie back into the wall. But the bricklayers in flint districts are clever at chipping the stuff into the best ways of jointing, and the squares of light and dark have a fine effect.

In so slight a survey of cottage construction it is impossible to notice the many ways of building all over Britain, but these few examples may suffice to point out to the general observer, and especially to any who have building projects in contemplation, how desirable it is in every district to make use of local material and to employ it as nearly as may be in the traditional manner ; but these few notes may be added. In the eastern counties where chalky soil prevails, walling is mostly of flint or brick and the roofs of pantiles, but in some places where the framing is of timber the panels are plastered and ornament is wrought in the plaster ; or the whole is plastered over, so giving scope for wider decorative treatment. Barns were commonly thatched, the work beautifully finished with a double cresting at the ridge. In Warwickshire and Worcestershire the older cottages are of half timber and are roofed with plain tiles or thatch. In Somerset and Devon there are cob walls, plastered and whitewashed, with the roofs heavily thatched. In Cheshire, Shropshire and Herefordshire, half timber prevails, with brick filling faced with plaster, and it is in these counties and nearby adjoining districts, but especially in Cheshire, that some of the finest timber walling was built. In the best examples there is upright studding below, followed by diagonal forms, and in the upper parts symmetrical arrangements of curved or cusped braces, with plastered brick filling. The roofs are of stone slates. In Kent, Sussex and Surrey, the walling of the older cottages was of timber with wattle or brick filling, and the roof of plain tiling or thatch, with in one district the stone slates known as Horsham slabs on the borders of Surrey and Sussex.

A few words may be said as to roofing ; there is no more comfortable roofing material than straw thatch—a non-conductor of both heat and cold. It is much to be feared that the art of thatching as applied to houses is dying out, now that easy communication brings tiles and slates from afar. But as it is receiving attention from architects it is to be hoped that this fine old roofing material may yet be saved, and that a younger generation of thatchers may be learning and practising the ancient art according to the several local ways. There is a general impression that thatch is in danger from fire and there may be some risk when it is quite fresh ; but this apprehension has been over-much magnified, for a thatched roof when matured is found to be not easily inflammable. Moreover, there are ways of spraying a newly thatched roof with a chemical solution that resists fire. It is regrettable that insurance companies either refuse to insure thatched buildings, or put on them so high a premium that the use of this fine roofing material is almost forbidden to those who would wish to make use of it.

In fenny districts a good thatch is made of reeds, but in speaking of thatching the word " reed " does not always mean a water plant, for in some places the straw prepared for thatching is called reed. There is also a durable thatch made in some of the home counties where there is much copse land, and where well-grown rods of hazel, ash and mountain ash are shaved on two sides in preparation for their being used as barrel hoops. The shavings, taken off with the draw-knife, are in strips that may be anything up to two feet long. They are called hoop chips and are tied in bundles and stacked to dry. They make a good thatch for all but the ridge which has to be of straw, for the chips are not long enough to bend over.

A sound thatch that lasts for many years is also made in moorland districts of the late-blooming heather. As the surface is less smooth than that of straw thatch it mosses over more quickly.

Where there is stone that splits into thin layers it is one of the best roofing materials, and one that has the best appearance. Such stones, as distinct from true slates, occur in many parts of England ; their colour, less cold and harsh than that of the grey and blue slates, is pleasant with a stone-built wall and their comparative irregularity also helps pictorial aspect. They are laid with the largest and heaviest next to the eaves, where the rafters have the strongest bearing, and decrease in width and thickness as they approach the ridge.

FIG. 123.—THE ALMSHOUSES, MAPLEDURHAM, OXFORDSHIRE.

FIG 124.—RUDHALL ALMSHOUSES, ROSS, HEREFORDSHIRE.

FIG. 125.—HALL'S ALMSHOUSES, BRADFORD-ON-AVON.

FIG. 127.——A THATCHED DORMER, SHIRBURN, OXFORDSHIRE.

FIG. 126.——THE ENTRANCE, HALL'S ALMSHOUSES

FIG. 128.—A COTTAGE AT FRENSHAM, SURREY.

FIG. 129 —A NEW COTTAGE, BUILT IN SURREY WITHOUT
RESTRICTIVE BYLAWS.

FIG. 130.—UNSTEAD FARM, GODALMING.

FIG. 131.—TILEHUNG COTTAGES, MILFORD, SURREY.

FIG. 132.—THE DAIRY COURT, UNSTEAD FARM.

FIG. 133.—AT ABBOTS WORTHY, HAMPSHIRE.

FIG. 134.—AT STEVENTON, BERKSHIRE.

98

FIG. 136.—WINDER.

FIG. 137.—SPINNING WHEEL.

FIG. 138.—WOMAN AT SPINNING WHEEL.

VII.

HOME INDUSTRIES.

FROM the earliest ages of which there is written record, spinning has been one of the most important of women's occupations. Archæologists tell us that the thick rings of stone or burnt pottery that have been found in many places where there are traces of the earliest known human habitations and are known as whorls, were the weights on the end of the spindle. Long before the spinning wheel was invented, spinning was done with the distaff and spindle only. The distaff is the rod that holds the bunch of prepared flax ; the lower end was supported in the woman's girdle. As she drew the thread she gave it a twist that set the spindle twirling ; the whorl, fixed to its lower end, increasing its weight and prolonging the spinning motion ; the thread was then wound on the spindle and temporarily held in a notch and the same thing went on again. This primitive way of producing a thread for weaving which has been practised from all ages of human civilization still goes on in rural places in Italy and other countries ; it has the advantage over the spinning wheel that the woman can work as she walks, or watches goats or sheep or cattle, whereas the more cumbersome wheel is only adapted for work within the dwelling. In the middle ages women of all classes used the spinning wheel—mistress and maids alike. Though it went on in Scotland and is in use there to this day in the case of woollen yarn for weaving and knitting, the use of the spinning wheel has practically died out in England, though it may still linger in the north. But in the earlier years of the nineteenth century home-grown flax was still prepared and spun by women in the southern counties, the industry dying out about the year 1830. Another of the earlier and most necessary of home works was the grinding of corn in the quern, a kind of stone mortar in which the corn was anciently pounded with another stone, and later crushed and reduced to a coarse meal by means of a convex stone that fitted loosely inside the hollow one and was turned by an iron or wooden handle fixed upright near the outer edge. The quern was used in England till the time of the Commonwealth, though

8

in its later days probably only for the grinding of malt, but its use for grinding corn for bread persisted much longer in the Highlands of Scotland.

Among the many gracious things belonging to the older days whose disuse we have reason to regret is the working of samplers. It may have been begun earlier, but from our actual knowledge of existing specimens we know that it went on for three hundred years, only coming to an end towards the middle of the nineteenth century. It is believed that the earlier specimens were the work of experienced needlewomen, but we know from what is actually shown on the later pieces that those of the eighteenth century at least were the work of children, some of quite tender age. There is an example in the national collection of a sampler worked and signed by a child of seven. An examination of one of these pieces shows what an excellent training it must have been to the young eye and hand.

The earlier examples were on long-shaped strips of linen covered with horizontal bands of alphabets, and either running border patterns or a succession of forms roughly square or diamond-shaped, treated with various fillings of symmetrical design. Later the form of the sampler was wider, more in the proportion of an upright picture, and the decorative needlework took forms of greater freedom and a wider play of fancy. A sampler dated 1764 in the writer's possession, measuring 18 by 13 inches, has, besides a number of small floral exuberancies that cannot be described, representations of the following objects :—Six pots or tubs of growing plants with foliage, fruit and flowers, all different ; a tree bearing fruit, with Adam and Eve and the Serpent ; two baskets of flowers quite differently treated ; a lady and gentleman with flowers in their hands ; a large iris fairly true to nature and near it a smaller heraldic fleur-de-lis ; three peacocks in different aspects, one with tail displayed ; a swan crowned ; a stork and several smaller birds ; a heraldic lion whose tail at intervals breaks out into foliated enrichment and ends in a volute of arabesque ; the Lamb and banner treated in two ways of different size ; the Cross with the Hebrew inscription, a crowing cock on a pillar and the implements of crucifixion ; a landscape with trees and what appears to be a terrace bordering water ; a castle, showing three rings of buildings rising on a mound ; a bird carrying a heart ; a lifelike carrot ; a built up well with cupola top and finials, and a hanging bucket ; a stag pursued by a hound ; a chair, a crown, another basket ; an object with two handles which looks like a *couvre-feu* ; here and there a couple of inches of running ornament ; the whole filled in with small matters such as jugs, tankards, and little sprays of fruit or flower. In the middle of the upper part is the signature M.R., enclosed in a floral border.

It seems evident that, though the earlier strip-shaped samplers were made as needlework patterns only, the later ones were intended to be framed as pictures; often they have an important floral border. Towards the end of the eighteenth century the sampler took another form—that of a map, but also as a picture for framing. One of these in the writer's possession, dated 1783, is a carefully done map of Europe; it is the more interesting because it has the original frame, (Fig. 140).

A poor woman living in an almshouse, who was known to the writer, had made a curious little picture of sampler character; a recollection of her earliest home; the side walls and their windows were shown in an odd way, in line with the front (Fig. 143). It must have been done about the year 1860.

Patchwork was done in many a thrifty home. Early in the nineteenth century women of the working classes wore, almost exclusively, gowns of cotton print with aprons and sunbonnets of the same; any odd pieces were saved to make a patchwork quilt. Some of these pieces of old work are interesting, not only for the taste and judgment shown in the pattern and arrangement of colours, but for the designs of the prints themselves; some examples in brown and purple were curiously waved and shaded, with a capital rich effect. It was a prize to get hold of a piece of flowered chintz as a centrepiece, and perhaps some of the same in the middle of the four sides of the bordering. It was treated with much respect, sometimes isolated by strips of white linen or by some light coloured print with a very faint design. These pieces of patchwork are delightfully sympathetic in that they show the striving for beauty in the minds of simple people, beauty often achieved in the shaping and putting together of the pretty prints of a hundred years ago. And we remember with pleasure how the minds of the workers were perfectly fresh and unspoilt, so that the intention of making something good to look at as well as useful was perfectly genuine and spontaneous. At the present day the masses of badly designed and cheaply got up wares of every kind, of ignoble form and detestable so-called ornament, have had the deplorable effect of destroying the natural sense of a desire for simple beauty, and have created a hankering after what is confused and meretricious. It is all the more delightful to come upon some little piece of quite original cottage work such as the bit of application (Fig. 146) that, from the character of the frame, one would judge to have been done quite early in the nineteenth century. It is in bits of coloured cloth with details of woollen embroidery. From the basket of cut grey cloth rises a grand bloom of auricula in two shades of red-purple; quite curiously lifelike. From the basket also rise sprays of rosebuds, bell-flowers, lilies and pansies, all quite out of scale, but serving to fill the space prettily and to play their secondary part as minor accessories to the dominating auricula. Four strawberries, also strikingly lifelike, repose on the brown cloth ground; they are internally padded to give an effect of rotundity and are flecked with little silken seeds. The doing of it must have given the worker the most genuine happiness, a joy that would have been all the more keenly felt had she known how much her pretty bit of work would be prized and admired a hundred years hence. The cottage kettle-holder, of a later date (Fig. 144), is another example of realistic treatment; worked in cross-stitch on canvas, it shows the kettle on the fire with a modern grate, mantelpiece and fender.

The washing of clothing and household linen was always, as now, a weekly duty. In the older days, much that is now done in a convenient wash-house or back kitchen was done out of doors in cold water; the soaped linen either slapped on a small stone or beaten with a wooden bat. The fixed copper with fire under, and the handy washtubs with hot and cold water taps over, was a much later invention and a great advance, while the clever washing machines now in use were undreamt of. The older smoothing irons, though like the later ones as to the body, had the handles more tipped forward, as seen in Fig. 145. In Scotland, in the old days, women trod in the wash-tub; it was called " tramping."

One wonders at the general modern neglect of that useful implement, the mop. Used wet it picks up dust or dirt from a floor of any material, and its restoration to use would save many a backache and much painful crawling about on knees.

It must be admitted that our cottage women are certainly less thrifty and industrious than those of the same class in continental countries, and it is rare to find them engaged in any special home work. It is true that some of them go out to work in the houses of more well-to-do people, but genuine home industries exist only in certain districts, such as the straw-plaiting in Bedfordshire, and lace-making in a few places. But a special need sometimes awakens local response, as in a case that occurred during the war. There was a great shortage in Hampshire of the rush baskets used as workmen's dinner baskets. The

FIG. 139.—PICTURE IN APPLICATION AND EMBROIDERY.

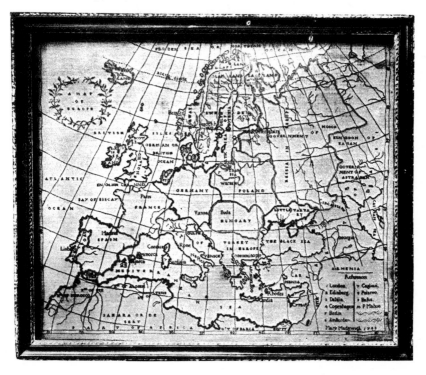

FIG. 140.—SAMPLER MAP OF EUROPE, 1783

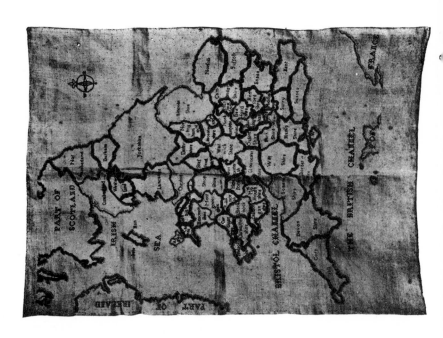

FIG. 143.—SMALL SQUARE SAMPLER.

FIG. 144.—KETTLE-HOLDER.

FIG. 145.—OLD SMOOTHING IRONS.

FIG. 146.—PATCHWORK QUILT, EARLY NINETEENTH CENTURY.

want was keenly felt in the district north of Winchester, and as the question of promoting some special industry arose in connection with the Institute in the village of Micheldever, it was decided that the making of these baskets should be their choice. A woman was found who knew and could teach the work ; it soon became a complete success and is now a thriving business. The material is a wild sedge which is dried and made into a plait of seven (Fig. 148.). It is a happy thing for England that such enterprises are being fostered throughout the land. No praise or congratulation can be too fervently offered to those who are giving thought and energy to the promoting of such a village industry. It not only provides something that is actually wanted and brings a welcome addition to the cottagers' weekly gains, but it stimulates industry and thrift and a wholesome spirit of emulation, not only in quantity of output but also in quality of workmanship.

VIII.

ROUND ABOUT THE FARM.

IT is a strange thing, and one of the most regrettable, but it seems to be a law with hardly any exception, that the new order that replaces the old brings with it unsightliness in place of the former comeliness. And though the re-awakening of a sense of beauty in matters concerning architecture, house decoration and furnishing and the arranging of gardens, among people of the more well-to-do classes has arisen to a new and better life, yet in all that pertains to the simple necessities of life and their production, is changing from its older beauty into something, in most cases, of positive ugliness. It is now rare indeed that, passing along country roads and through villages, anything new is to be seen that has any kind of attractive appearance. So it is also in and about the farm. If a new farm building is wanted it is roofed, if not wholly constructed, of corrugated iron. What a miserable contrast to the simple old building such as the one shown (Fig.170) with granary above and shelter for carts and waggons below. In the more advanced farming, mechanical traction is taking the place of horse power. Perhaps a few years hence we shall no longer see the jolly teams of horses starting out for the day's work or see them at work in the field or carrying the loads of farm produce along the roads. Are we to expect the extinction of those splendid breeds of heavy horses—the grand Shires and the powerful Suffolks ? Is all this living strength and beauty to give way to dead contrivances of unsightly iron ? (Fig. 150.)

The wooden plough with its beautiful lines of arching beam and stilts, of a pattern that has endured more or less unchanged for hundreds of years, is still in use and well liked in some remote districts, but will never be made again ; its place has been taken by one entirely of iron, even if any plough at all survives for horse draught. Still older and more pictorial was the use of bullock teams for ploughing and all farm work. Now it is to be feared that these are quite extinct, though they lingered among the Berkshire and Sussex Downs till well within living memory.

The whole of the operations of haymaking were formerly entirely beautiful and it was a season of joyful labour in high summertide. All the farm folk, men and women alike, worked in the field from daylight to dusk. The mowers were followed by the women who shook out the grass for the first day's drying and at short intervals was heard the ringing music of the stone on the scythe blade ; the whetstone, commonly called a rubber, was carried in a leather loop at the back of the man's waistbelt. A good mower would cut an acre in a day. The regular meals were many, but the work was hard. They had breakfast at six, lunch at half-past nine, dinner at noon, afternoon lunch at four, and supper at seven. The women would make a fire and boil a kettle for the four o'clock meal.

Fig. 147.—OLD SUSSEX WOODEN PLOUGH.

In some hilly districts and awkward places where it was impossible to take a cart, a low, rough truck was used for carrying hay, as illustrated in Fig. 162. It had a pair of axles and four solid wooden wheels not larger than a small dinner plate. An even more primitive thing was also in use : a kind of sledge without wheels, a rough framework of branches only.

The later corn harvest was another of the year's festivals of labour, when all the wheat was reaped by hand. It was a time of general gladness and thankfulness and benefit to labouring folk ; not in wages only, but also in kind, for the farmer was liberal in his treatment of his men's families in the matter of gleaning. In Pyne's " Microcosm," that clear mirror of the working life of a hundred years ago, we read this about gleaning : " We recollect a spectacle of this sort on the fields of an extensive farmer of the old cast. The children of his cottagers, in great number, with males and females too old or infirm to reap, would keep close up with those who bound the sheaves behind the reaper, and sometimes pass them. The harshest thing that this patriarchal head of the hamlet, who was revered and in a manner adored by his numerous people, would say was, ' Children, you must not come too near,' or ' Don't take out of the sheaves.' A family of four or five children, with a mother who could only spare a few hours occasionally, or a feeble grandfather, would frequently at the end of the harvest find from six to ten bushels of wheat, with a proportionate quantity of barley and oats, provided for the winter." These happy and bountiful, busy and yet fairly leisurely days, are good to think back upon, and a pleasant contrast to our present conditions when the corn is reaped and bound and the sheaves tossed aside by a clattering machine.

To the middle of the nineteenth century and for hundreds of years before, the corn was stored in the barn and threshed out by hand with the flail. Now there is no longer a use for barns, those noble and gracious buildings, with their stored wealth of food for man and beast, for the corn is stacked in the field and threshed and winnowed together by a steam engine ; nor is there now so much use for the rick settle, or staddle as it is called in some parts, with its stone posts and their mushroom-shaped caps for the prevention of rat invasion. Some of the old barns that remain and especially the tithe barns attached to the religious houses are a wonder and delight to all who can feel the nobility of simple architecture. The great tithe barn at Tisbury, in Wiltshire, one of the buildings of an apanage to the Abbey of Shaftesbury, still stands (Fig. 167) ; the roof a great example of the use of timber. The slightly cambered beams, with their giant braces only stopping a short distance from each other form a series of noble arches, all the more satisfying to the structural sense from the consciousness of there being a stout buttress against each on the outer side of the solid stone wall.

Not the plough only, but all the old tools belonging to the corn have gone out of use. The dibbling irons, when seed was carefully sown by hand, were used one in each hand by a man walking backwards over the field, so making two lines of holes (see Fig 165) ; he was followed by children who dropped a grain or two in each hole. It was said that dibbled wheat was finer than any other. The reaping hook, following the still older sickle, is dead also (see Fig. 166). The sickle differed from the reaping hook in that the blade was transversely grooved, the ends of the grooves coming to the cutting edge, so that the edge was actually a saw, exactly like

FIG. 149.—USE OF THE MOP ABOUT 1820.

FIG. 148.—PLAITING RUSHES.

FIG. 150.—A SUFFOLK HORSE.

FIG. 151.—THE MODERN TRACTOR.

FIG. 152.—A BULLOCK TEAM CARTING HAY.

FIG. 153.—" SEED TIME," SHOWING THE USE OF THE WOODEN PLOUGH.

From the Painting by J. F. Herring, 1854-56.

FIG. 154.—A WOODEN PLOUGH.

FIG. 155.—THE HURDLE MAKER.

FIG. 156 —FOUR-HORSE TEAM CARTING SACKS.

FIG. 157.—FIVE-HORSE TEAM HARROWING.

FIG. 158.—SHORTHORN BULLOCK TEAM ON THE BERKSHIRE DOWNS.

FIG. 159.—LOADING AND CARTING HAY.

FIG. 160.—THE MOWER.

FIG. 161.—PLOUGHING WITH A FOUR-HORSE TEAM.

FIG. 162.—A HAY TRUCK.

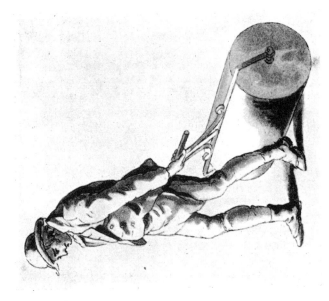

FIG. 164.—STONE GARDEN ROLLER.

FIG. 163.—GLEANERS.

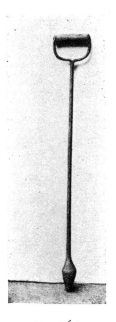

FIG. 165.
DIBBLING IRON.

FIG 166.—REAPING HOOKS AND FAG HOOK.

FIG. 167 —A TITHE BARN, TISBURY, WILTSHIRE.

FIG. 168.—DETAIL OF FLAIL HEAD.

FIG. 169.—THRESHING.

FIG. 170.—GRANARY AND WAGGON SHED.

FIG. 171 —A COTTAGER'S BEEHIVES.

FIG. 172.—SMITHS MAKING HAY RAKES, CHESHIRE.

FIG. 173.—DORSET SMITHS AT WORK.

that of a toothing plane. Why this was given up it is not easy to perceive for to this day the country labourer keeps his fag-hook hung up in the cottage porch or somewhere where the edge may rust. The inequality so caused gives the tool an edge not unlike that of the sickle. The fag-hook is a heavier tool than the reaping hook and is always at hand for such purposes as the trimming of rough hedges. It is used with a different action, for whereas the reaping hook was drawn across the straw with a dragging stroke, the fag-hook is a slashing tool.

The flail was one of the oldest of the farmers' implements. It is formed of two rods about 3 feet 6 inches long, the handle being the slighter and the swingel the thicker and heavier. The loop head of the handle is formed of a bit of tough green ash, thinned in the middle and cut into two square shoulders at the ends. It is bent over so that the shoulders meet or nearly meet, and were made to fit loosely round an iron pin just under its wide, flat head, so that the whole of the ash hoop could revolve easily. The two shoulders when brought together are firmly bound with saddlers' waxed twine. The fitting of the iron pin is a neat bit of blacksmith's work, but all the rest is made on the farm. The swingel (the " g " is soft as in " angel ") has an end loop of raw hide, bound on with the same, and another loose loop of raw hide puts the two together. There may be many yet living who can remember the pleasing sight and sound of threshing ; the man's dexterity, for there were labourers who would undertake to knock all the grain out of a single head of corn stood up on end at the first blow, and the pleasant sound, the " whish " when the flail first struck the loose corn, and the thump when, after a few strokes, the heavy swingel felt the floor.

Many thrifty cottagers keep bees, and though advanced bee-masters use the more scientific wooden hives (see Fig. 171), with their convenient ways of inserting and withdrawing the sections, yet the old people cling to the straw hive ; moreover, a straw hive, easily carried, is a convenient thing in which to take a swarm that has settled within reach. Some cottagers make their own hives in the winter of untwisted ropes of straw bound or stitched together with bands made of thin strips of willow or hazel or even of bramble. When a swarm comes over, the old people think to attract it and induce it to settle by some sort of metallic noise, such as rattling a stick in a tin can, but the old established formula was the beating of a plough-share with a heavy door-key. Hives of bees should have some kind of shelter or covering ; in the picture the cottage people have supplied this and at the same time made the thing well looking with two old sacks and the two halves of a broken redware pan (Fig. 171).

9

There are several old superstitions connected with bees. One is that whenever anyone begins to keep them, the first stock must never be bought—it must be a free gift. Another that prevails in many parts is that when there is a death in the cottage, one of the first duties is to go out and tell the bees. These customs vary much in different parts of the country.

Beer was brewed in every farm a hundred years ago, and often in the labourer's cottage, but was generally discontinued about the second decade of the nineteenth century. Cider making was general in all country districts till quite recently. It is a matter for regret that it should have ceased to be made in any district as it is an excellent and most wholesome drink. A study has lately been made of the best French methods—Normandy and Brittany are great cider countries—and it is to be hoped that the industry may be generally revived. The main centres of cider making in Herefordshire, Gloucestershire, and Devon are not likely to decrease their output, for their excellent ciders are in constant demand.

The farm has always been a good customer to the forge, for apart from the ever busy shoeing shed the smith's yard was often full of waggons and various implements wanting repair or renewal. A smith in a rather large way would have a separate shop for the wheelwright in his employment, for the two trades hang together (Figs. 172, 173); but many of the smaller men were handy with woodwork also, and if work at the forge was slack they would turn to and make hay rakes or anything for which there was a local demand. Hoes for farm and garden are always wanted, and were made when other work was not urgent. There is generally, in every district, a smith who has a special reputation for turning out good hoes.

Wattle hurdles for folding sheep, as shown in Fig. 155, were, and still are, made in the copses in the winter and early spring. The hurdle maker would go from place to place, cut the hazel and fashion the hurdles. His only tool is the handbill, and his only other appurtenance the hurdle frame. This is a block of wood a little over six feet in length, slightly curved, but only curved enough for it to remain upright. It has a hole right through at the two ends and shallower holes at intervals between. The end ones hold the end uprights; they are the stoutest in all its structure; the inner uprights take the horizontal rods, usually split in half, that are woven in and out and pass round the outer stake with a clever twist that opens the fibres and forms a kind of tough rope. A space is left in the middle for the shepherd to carry the hurdle by hand, or he will put two or three together, pass a stake through and carry them on his back.

The very old industry of charcoal burning still goes on in the woods, though not so extensively as formerly. The men make rough shelters and camp close to the work, for the smouldering heaps have to be watched night and day.

The old labourers who could neither read nor write had various ways of setting down the amount of work done and of presenting their bills. The present writer has had a

Fig. 174.—A BRICKLAYER'S BILL.

hazel stick inscribed with a certain arrangement of notches and crosses showing work carried out on a job of thatching, but a more curious example is the one illustrated—a bill for 10s. 10d. from a bricklayer. It means that two men and one boy worked three-quarters of a day and used two hods of mortar. The two crosses are the signature and the figure hanging means that the bill is settled. Its date is somewhere near 1815.

The stone garden roller, though not necessarily a farm implement, deserves some record. It was in use till near the middle of the nineteenth century; after that it was often cleared of its iron handle and set up as a shaft for a sundial or other garden ornament.

The days are past when the harvest feast was one of the few country holidays, but they were days of real enjoyment, not only to the farm people, but to many of the local residents who came to rejoice with them. There was plenty of good food and drink and dancing to the music of pipe and fiddle. The men's hats were wreathed with flowers. The illustration from an old print (Fig. 175), gives a good idea of the simple happiness of this joyous festival. The other chief occasion for festivity was May Day, when all classes joined together to make a long day of happy holiday and reasonable revelry. For hundreds of years this happy spring festival had been kept, and its continuance went on till well into the nineteenth century. The Maypole was raised, or possibly stood, from year to year; it was decorated with wreaths and streamers of ribbon and was the centre of traditional dances. A May Queen was chosen and crowned; she sat in state near the Maypole in a bower of green branches. In the early morning the young people went maying and returned laden with branches of hawthorn bloom and with flowers in their hats. Then the whole day was given to feasting and dancing (see illustration, Fig. 176). This holiday and that of the Harvest Home were the chief days of rural rejoicing, other than the occurrence of the yearly fairs of the towns and larger villages and the days connected with Church Festivals. There are modern attempts to revive the Maypole and its attendant festivities, but the thing does not ring true. It is created from without instead of being something spontaneous from within. The continuous chain of ancient tradition has been snapped and nothing can restore it.

The present writer can remember one of the last links of the old May Day doings—the chimney sweeps' Jack-in-the-Green. It was still to be seen in the streets of London in the late forties of the nineteenth century. The eight-foot-high tower of greenery dancing in a lumbering way and sometimes completely revolving was a matter of awful mystery to the small child; of wonder, of intense curiosity, and of some fear. In country places some May Day observances lingered to within the last few years. They may still survive in remote places, but are practically extinct in the Home Counties. But fifty years ago it was usual for village children to come round on May Day with bunches of flowers bound on the tops of peeled willow sticks, and some with an intersecting double ring of hoops of flowers and foliage carried by two children on a horizontal stick. It was accompanied by a continued monotonous chant of " The first of May is Garland Day, so please to remember the white wand ; we don't come here but once a year, so please to remember the Garland." It was all on one note except that the last but one syllable jumped up three tones.

FIG. 175.—AN EIGHTEENTH CENTURY HARVEST CELEBRATION.

From a Contemporary Print.

FIG. 176.—A MAYPOLE DANCE IN THE SIXTEENTH CENTURY.

From a Watercolour by Joseph Nash, 1854.

FIG. 178.—THE SUNBONNET, WIGMORE, HEREFORDSHIRE.

FIG. 177.—" THE MILKWOMAN " (CRIES OF LONDON).
By F. Wheatley, R.A.

FIG. 180.—THE SUNDAY BONNET.

FIG. 179.—THE COTTAGE CAP.

IX.

OLD PEOPLE AND COSTUME.

ONE of our serious losses of the present day is that of the simple and useful dress of the working people of a hundred years ago, and especially of the tidy and becoming caps of the women. The head kerchief, still commonly worn on the Continent, the most clean, cheap and practical of head coverings, was never adopted in England, neither was there anything representing the distinctive headdresses of different though closely connected districts as in Brittany. But the white cap, amply covering the back of the head, with a band and slightly frilled front that was prolonged into a flap covering the ears and ended in short strings, to be tied or not under the chin, was the unfailing headgear of women and girls. A flat-shaped hat of black felt was worn over the cap on such occasions as market days and at Church, but the cap alone sufficed for ordinary wear. There was a short bodice fastened either at back or front. sometimes with a lacing ; a stout petticoat and over it a skirt drawn up under itself so that it formed a bunchy " panier " over the hips and at the back, and then an apron. The bodice was cut low at the top all round, leaving the neck widely bare in summer, or covered with a kerchief of cotton or woollen, according to the season. A loose, warm cloak with a hood was worn with the hat, or when the hat was omitted, with the hood drawn over the head. The picture of a London milkwoman (Fig. 177) shows this charming costume at its, best but a debased but yet characteristic dress was worn in London within the memory of those still living by the women who still delivered milk. They carried the milk in the old way in two large pails with a yoke, and wore a short-skirted print gown, thick boots, and a woollen shoulder kerchief. A straw bonnet of the country pattern was usually worn tipped forward so that the part that should be at the back came over the crown of the head. Some such dress as that of the picture went on till about 1830, when there came the change to bonnets and shawls ; the pretty bunched panier was left off and the cotton gown was made, sometimes all in one, or with a separate skirt and loose jacket bodice. Many of the cotton prints from this and the earlier time, as we see from

10

existing patchwork quilts, were of beautiful and curious design ; some that are specially interesting were in clouded shadings of pink, purple, or brown.   The sunbonnets worn in some districts, and still in use in the West Country (see illustration, Fig. 178), were always charming. When the loose white cap of the earlier quarter of the century went out, its place was taken by a cap of coarse muslin fitting close to the head called the caul, with a stiff frill of cotton lace framing the face, as shown in Fig. 179.   It had a ribbon just behind the frill that passed over the head and tied under the chin.   It was becoming to an honest country face, and the starched frill formed a fresh looking finish to the bonnet that went with it.   The pride of the cottage house-wife was the Sunday bonnet of black satin (Fig. 180).   It was made with several rows of drawn work, something after the manner of the main part of the sunbonnet, but stiffened and widening a little at the front.   It had a curtain at the back and was finished with a bow of the same black satin at the top.   This bonnet, with a plain black shawl and a clean starched print gown was the usual Sunday dress of the better class of cottager, and was general till near the year 1860.

The clothing of the men in the early 19th century was a long-cut coat, with waistcoat and knee breeches, and for cold or wet weather a full length greatcoat with a wide cape over the shoulders.   Thick stockings and low shoes completed the usual leg-gear.   For some kinds of work loose leather spats were worn over the shoes.   One wonders at the absence of the comfortable and convenient ankle boots that did not come into use till later, also of leather gaiters which seem to have been only worn by slaughtermen or gamekeepers.   The round frock of stout linen was the labourer's common wear in place of a coat.   One kind of hat appears to have been general (Fig. 184) ; straight and low in the crown, with a wide brim that tipped and bent in all directions.   It is easy to see how such a hat, in other classes and professions, took varying forms.   The brim fastened up at three points made the neat three-cornered hat ; drawn up at the sides it would be the forerunner of the staff officer's cocked hat ; fixed up back and front the headgear of Napoleon and of some of the home regiments of the day.   The modern ugly but no doubt efficient braces were never worn.   It may be supposed that they came in with the later trousers.   That excellent garment, the fisherman's jersey, was unknown, though it was probably in use in France.   From its name we may suppose that it came to us from France through the Channel Islands.   A woollen cap of night-cap shape was commonly used by fishermen and longshoremen.   Distinctive dresses

FIG. 181.—THE CARTER'S SMOCK.

FIG. 182.—AN OPEN-AIR MARKET A CENTURY AGO.

FIG. 183.—CASTLE RISING ALMSHOUSES, NORFOLK

FIG 185.—AN OLD WELSHWOMAN.

FIG. 184.—BOY IN OLD SMOCK, CHESHIRE.

FIG. 186.—OLD SUNDAY SMOCK.

FIG. 187.—HANDKERCHIEF BUNDLES.

were worn by various trades, such as that of the Thames watermen. Nearly all are now lost ; all, in fact, except such a matter of necessity as the smith's leather apron. But as recently as the year 1860 carpenters still wore a short jacket of thick white baize, and it is only of late years that we have lost the red caps of the brewers' draymen.

Distinctive costume lingered only in more remote or backward places. The knee breeches and low shoes, the common wear of all the country till about the year 1820, remained in Ireland for another forty years. The woman's steeple-crowned hat of the seventeenth and eighteenth centuries survived in Wales, and has now become the typical national headdress, though its present use may be more of an artificial resurrection than a true survival (Fig. 189). But it has always been preserved and still remains, with the red cloak bearing the badge of the Howards, as a part of the costume of the inmates of the Castle Rising Almshouses in Norfolk, built by the Earl of Arundel in the seventeenth century (Fig. 183).

The carter's round frock or smock-frock, as shown Figs. 181, 184 and 186), remained in general use till past the middle of the nineteenth century. It was a capital thing for all country purposes. Its shape varied very little, only, in fact, in the size and form of the short cape or collar. The smocking arose as a necessity of construction, for neither body nor sleeves were cut into shape. The lengths of stout, close woven linen were left full width, and the smocked portions occurred where the fulness was drawn up into close gathers, and was treated in various devices of clever needlework. This close gathering, though apparently chiefly ornamental, was of distinct utility, the much increased thickness giving protection to the back and chest, and whereas the whole garment would turn a surprising amount of wet, the smocked portions were almost impervious to rain. The word " smock " has an interesting and ancient derivation from an Icelandic word meaning a garment or anything with a hole that the head can be put through. Later, in England it was used exclusively for a woman's shift, and we have it in the old name for the Cuckoo-flower or Ladies'-smock, a name whose sense it is easy to follow, because a mass of these nearly white flowers in a meadow may well resemble washed linen laid out to dry or bleach. Later still, the name came down to this shirt-like outer frock for men, but it is only quite recently that the word has been made into a verb and applied to this class of ornamental needlework.

Fortunately, nothing is ever likely to supersede those two splendid cotton materials, corduroy and fustian.   The old labourer resting by the roadside in the picture (Fig. 188) is clothed in these.   They have the merit that is shared by every thoroughly good woven stuff, of never looking shabby however much wear they may have had.   They may be worn and stained by many a long day's labour, but the man looks well dressed to the last because the stuff and making of his clothes are exactly suited to his life and work.   He wears cord trousers, and the sleeved waistcoat that has the front of cord and the sleeves and back of fustian.   Such clothing cannot be beaten for comfort and utility, and the farm labourer knows their value.

It is curious to note how old traditions of clothing persist among fishing people.   One of the few places where the Welsh hat is genuinely worn is by the fish women of Llangwm, in Pembrokeshire, who walk many miles to bring oysters and prawns to Tenby and other neighbouring places (Fig. 189).   They also wear their old costume on the occasion of Church Festivals.   The Carmarthenshire cockle woman has her underskirt pulled up by a string that passes between the legs (shown in Fig. 190), and the cockle gatherers on the East Coast fasten up their skirts in exactly the same way.   It is, no doubt, the traditional manner of arranging their clothing to suit their work, though it seems strange, considering the long hours they work at raking the cockles out of the sand, that they should not have adopted some kind of short skirt better suited to the work, without so much bunching and contriving.   We are all familiar with the beautiful old costume of the Boulogne fish women ; a dress that can never be seen without admiration.

Country people did not travel much from fifty to a hundred years ago, but when they did their small amount of personal baggage was done up in the large, yard-square handkerchiefs known as carrying kerchiefs and shown in Fig. 187.   Within the last twenty years they were yet to be had in country clothing shops, but now, as they are still used by sailors, they are more easily had in seaport towns.   But in the old days they were commonly used for all kinds of light carrying, for shopping and weekly marketing, conveniently supplementing a capacious basket, and for many of the purposes for which we now use paper and string.

FIG 190.—A CARMARTHENSHIRE COCKLEWOMAN.

FIG. 189.—AN OYSTER WOMAN, LLANGWM, PEMBROKESHIRE.

140

FIG. 191.—THE PEDLARS.

FIG. 192.—THE GYPSIES' CAMP FIRE.

From Aquatints by J. B. Pyne.

X.

TRAVELLING TRADERS AND GYPSIES.

IN the eighteenth century and earlier, and well into the nineteenth, the pedlar, or packman as he was formerly more usually called, was always a popular person, and was well received at the farms (see illustration, Fig. 191). His roving life gave him an open mind, a shrewd insight into human nature, and a wide sympathy with his fellow creatures. His visits occurring year after year, he was well known to the farmer and respected for his honest dealing. Often he would stay more than one night, helping in the farm work by day, and in the evenings entertaining his hosts with song and story. The better class of packman travelled with a horse and panniers, but the greater number of them went on foot, with a leather box of goods slung on the back, or held in front when it was opened to display the wares. In the more remote districts especially, the packman's visits were a boon to the housewife, for he brought small things like needles and thread, tapes and buttons and other things among the minor items of haberdashery such as are so often wanted in cottage and farmhouse.

The travelling tailor was another welcome visitor, staying at the farm till his work was done, for the farmer bought his cloth as he had the opportunity in the large town and waited for the tailor's visit to have it made up. Like the packman, the tailor, travelling from house to house —but his work lying within the smaller area of one district—heard all the local gossip and was the natural medium of its communication.

The rat-catcher (see Fig. 195) always found work at the farms ; his wire cage of rats and often a few more slung about him and his dog proclaiming his business when on the road. His ferret, as in the old picture, is of monstrous size, and must have been drawn from the artist's recollection rather than from nature.

The travelling chair-mender, though not entirely extinct, is now only rarely seen ; nor is he much wanted, for the comfortable rush-bottomed chairs of the older days are not so much in use as formerly, when they were in every farm and cottage, but it is always pleasant to see him at work sitting by the cottage door, or on the road carrying his " bolt " of rushes (see Fig. 196).

The knife-grinder is also becoming rare, though in former days his work was always in demand ; moreover, his modern equipment is less good to look at. But in the older days he had the heavy ash-framed barrow, as shown in Fig. 197, that carried the simple but effective machinery of his trade. A treadle worked the large, heavy wheel whose grooved edge transmitted the power by a band to the spindle on which the grindstone was set. After a few revolutions the weight of the wheel regulated and partly kept up the power, so that but little effort of his footwork was required. There are still a few knife-grinders about and these are almost the only remainder of these useful workmen who formerly frequented the roads. Now, much that was done on the spot—from house to house—the grinding of knives, scissors and razors—owing to the greater facilities of communication is sent to the nearest ironmonger, who packs it off to the larger centres to be done in bulk.

For the same reason the travelling tinker with his donkey cart is no longer seen. The front of his cart had a raised framework, under which is the bellows that gives a draught to a pan of charcoal (see illustration, Fig. 198). The bellows are worked by a lever, whose handle extends towards the back of the cart, where the man sits or stands. He has a small vice and an anvil, as well as a grindstone. These itinerant workmen must have made a good living and well deserved, it for they were clever craftsmen, and though their charges were low, their employment was fairly constant ; besides, they were often given food, especially in out of the way places.

Gypsies and other van dwellers still live by various small trades ; either by the retailing of such things as brooms and brushes or more often by the sale of the baskets that they make as they encamp, and small things such as clothes pegs (see Figs. 192 to 194). The baskets are mostly of split willow, with handles of ash or hazel. A distinction should be made between the true Romany and the rougher van-dweller, who is by no means always a real gypsy. The right people have a pleasant address and manner much like that of the Italian peasant ; they are generally honest, and have a good deal of self-respect. It is to be regretted that they have to so large an extent given up their distinctive dress ; the bright handkerchiefs for head and shoulders, and the long gold earrings. Now they dress in any old clothes that may be given to them, and wear on their heads any battered old hat with draggled feathers.

FIG. 193.—GYPSIES IN DORSET.

FIG. 194.—A GYPSY CARAVAN IN LINCOLNSHIRE.

FIG. 196.—THE CHAIRMENDER.

From Aquatints by J. B. Pyne.

FIG. 195.—THE RATCATCHER.

FIG. 197.—THE KNIFE-GRINDER.

FIG. 198.—THE TRAVELLING TINKER.

From Aquatints by J. B. Pyne.

FIG. 200.—THE OLD HURDY-GURDY.

FIG. 199.—THE WANDERER'S COOKING FIRE.

But there is always something attractive about the gypsy encampment. Unless they have a capacious van, the tent is still the low semi-circle of bent hazel rods covered with old blankets ; and they have a natural aptitude for choosing a pretty place for their temporary homes. The life must be a wholesome one, for the bare-footed and bare-headed children look strong and healthy.

XI.

SOME OLD COUNTRY MECHANISM.

IF we have gained by the use of modern machinery in rapidity and volume of production we have certainly lost in the comeliness of some of the objects of daily life. We go into some machine shed or power house and see certain engines, but their purpose and manner of working are not apparent to the ordinary observer, whereas in the earlier mechanical contrivance the whole story of the thing is plain to see ; the simple working is obvious to every beholder and therefore personally interesting.

The strong two-handled well winch, as shown in Fig. 203, of the earlier days of the nineteenth century needs no explanation ; it is protected from the weather by a wooden casing that has a certain refinement of outline, and the two steps lead up pleasantly to the point at which the heavy bucket has to be lifted down. The great wheel acts as a fly-wheel, regulating the power and increasing the momentum.

The hand pump of the same date illustrated in Fig. 202 has also some good lines in its simple structure and its little roof. The handle is of wood, and the leaden spout delivers the water into a dipping tank. Such a pump is to be seen to-day in many a foreign country town and village, where the conveniently central position of the public water supply becomes a place for daily meeting and local gossip.

There are many English valley villages where the cottages have wells of moderate depth and the old form of winch is used with a chain and pail. The illustration in Fig. 201 shows the most usual construction. Two courses of brickwork come out of the ground and a beam is set on two of the outer edges. Two posts, mortised into the beam at the bottom, are made rigid by a couple of stout braces ; a capping of two boards shoots off the main of the wet from the chain coiled on the axle. Danger to children is guarded against by a hinged flap that shuts down over the opening when the well is not in use ; a wooden catch holds it when it is open. In the case of quite shallow wells the pail is dipped at the end of a long pole with a spring hook that holds the handle.

FIG. 2OI.——THE COTTAGE WELL WINCH.

FIG. 203.—TWO-HANDLED WINCH.

From Aquatints by J. B. Pyne.

FIG. 202.—THE VILLAGE PUMP.

Where the well was deep, and greater strength than hand work was needed, some form of horse power was used. Many of us are acquainted with the patient donkey that plods round in the great wheel that raises the water in the deep well at Carisbrooke Castle in the Isle of Wight, illustrated in Fig. 205 pulling up a heavy bucket that is as big as his whole body. A contrivance of the same kind in miniature was the dog-wheel for turning a roasting spit—already described at page 25. Another adaptation of dog power is shown in the picture on page 147 of a diagonal wheel, in which the good dog going constantly uphill works a churn inside the Welsh farm dairy. It is to be hoped that he is well rewarded when the butter " comes."

When cider was made in quantity the apples were ground by horse power ; the illustration (Fig. 207) shows an old Devonshire cider mill with a horse gear in a covered place. The massive stone revolves in a trough in the solid stone cistern. The mechanism is not only admirably simple and effective, but also satisfying to the eye. The solid beam, curved where it passes over the horse's back, is braced to the central post with a wooden strut at the inner angle and iron stays above and below. The stone is set with a diagonal tilt corresponding to the slight slant in the bottom of the trough by which the pulp is conveyed to the middle outlet. The rim of the cistern is strongly hooped with iron. Some of the older mills had an arrangement of two stones, also with a horse gear, and the work was carried out quite in the open.

In the home counties cider is still made in small quantities by cottagers, but judging from the derelict presses seen occasionally, by no means so often as formerly. The mill was a wide trough slanting down to a thick wooden roller furrowed longitudinally, something after the manner of a millstone. The apples were pressed by hand against the roller, which was fixed in an open bench at a convenient height. A handle operating a larger cogged wheel that engaged with a smaller on the end of the roller, was the power. The crushed pulp fell into a tub set under the bench. The pulp then went into bags of coarse fibre that were stacked one over another in the press. The press was a solid structure of oak, sometimes a fixture in the orchard. Two solid, wide posts were planted in the ground like gateposts ; there was a thick and wide crosspiece on which the bags rested, with two great tenons that passed through the post and were secured with wedges. The head, about four feet up, was still more massive and took one end of the screw with a corresponding thread. At the lower end of the screw was a heavy wooden bob perforated both ways for the insertion of the lever that worked it after the manner of a capstan.   A thick block of wood, filling the whole space between the posts, and the same width as the platform on which the bags rested, was gradually forced down upon the bags. At every turn of the screw the juice flowed out and ran into a tub below. It was usual for an interested onlooker to be offered a mug of the fresh pressed juice, and though nothing very pleasant was anticipated, for the apples were only the second rate produce of the orchard and by no means special cider apples, and they went into the mill many of them bruised and muddy, yet it was surprising to find in the result a sweet and most palatable drink.

Cheesemaking was usual in the farms.   The cheese press was a massive squared stone hanging by an iron rod from the crosspiece of a wooden framework for lowering on to the cheese on the stone slab below (see illustration, Fig. 206).

The same kind of wooden-framed mechanism, whether large or small, was in use throughout the country a hundred years ago.   Great cranes for loading from timber stacks, or from wharf to barge or ship, were, all but their chains and hooks and bolts, of ponderous balks of oak ; the contrivances for hauling up fishing boats, planted above high-water mark, were alike of heavy timber ; everything plain and solid, simple and well-looking, revealing its purpose at a glance and showing the direct application of local intelligence to local need.

There are still existing here and there examples of a long pole with a hook at the end (as shown in Fig. 209) for tearing burning thatch off a house roof and even for pulling down timber-framed buildings to prevent fire from spreading.   The illustration shows a more powerful rude mechanism for the same purpose.   The hooked end of the long lever clutches the burning thatch, lowered by the men in front of the machine who haul on the chains.   When a good grip is secured the chains are let go, the counterbalance of the heavy end of the beam raises a good portion of the blazing thatch, and the machine is drawn back to allow it to be deposited clear of the house.

FIG. 204.—A DOGWHEEL ON A WELSH FARM.

FIG. 205.—THE WELL, CARISBROOKE CASTLE.

154

FIG. 206.—A CHEESE PRESS, KEGWORTH, LEICESTERSHIRE, NOW DESTROYED.

FIG. 207.—HORSE-DRIVEN CIDER MILL, DEVONSHIRE.

FIG. 208.—A TWO-STONE CIDER MILL.

FIG. 209.—MACHINE FOR DRAGGING OFF BURNING THATCH.

FIG. 210.—THE DOVECOTE, HARLESTONE, NEAR NORTHAMPTON.

XII.

MILLS AND DOVECOTES.

ONE of the dying features of the countryside that we have to deplore is the general disuse and falling into decay of the windmill. As in the case of all the other mechanical devices of the older times, when local material was adapted to local needs by the men of the place, the windmill grew into a thing of beauty through the simple necessities of its use and construction. The older form was known as the post mill, for a great post passed up the vertical axis of the building as far as the first floor and was firmly fixed at the base by diagonal stays resting on a masonry foundation; the whole mill revolves upon this at the floor line. Such a mill, dating from the early part of the seventeenth century, is the one at Nutley, in Sussex. The four sails are not upright but lean back at the top towards the mill, so that the powerful axle, which by cogged wheels conveys the power to the stones, has an inclination to the horizon of from eight to fifteen degrees. The fact of the sails being so set back brings the top of the uppermost sail well within the diameter of the plan of the roof, and thus throws a part of the weight well back, so diminishing the whole forward pull of the sails. Then the wooden steps that give access to the mill and the long lever known as the tailbeam, which are on the side of the mill furthest from the sails, form a nearly equivalent counterpoise, which both steadies the structure and satisfies the eye when viewing the mill in profile.

Later, mills were built solid from the ground in stone or brick, something like the stump of a lighthouse, and were known as tower mills. In this case the main body of the mill is fixed and only the top revolves. Attached to the top and set well out from it on the side furthest from the sails is a powerful circular vane, which adjusts the face of the sails to the direction of the wind. There are also various niceties of construction, all arising out of the necessity of conforming to natural law, such as the drawing in of the ends of the sails to a narrower width where the wind has more power, thus to equalise the wind's pressure and leverage, that add much to the sense of good " drawing " that in these old mills so keenly attracts the artist's eye.

Even the water flour mills that were formerly in every valley where there was anything like a rapid stream are going out of use. In quiet country places, the pond above the mill, with its fringes of reed and bulrush—the nesting place of moorhens—its alders and willows and its store of fish, was in itself an attractive spot. Then came the mill, with its pleasant murmur, that at a little distance told of its patient work in the preparation of our food, and then, in the actual building, all the interesting details of its structure and working (see Fig. 212). The mill is in three floors ; the sacks of grain are hoisted to the top floor where the corn is cleaned. It then descends by a hopper and shoot to the middle floor, and here are the millstones, enclosed in a wooden casing. The lower stone is fixed, the upper rotates upon it, not quite touching, but near enough to grind the corn, which gradually passes along the grooves that lead to its outer edge. From there it passes by another shoot to a bin on the ground floor. The wheel is just outside the lower floor of the mill ; its ponderous axle is prolonged and passes through the wall, ending in a powerful cog wheel which engages with a smaller, horizontal wheel to turn the spindle that passes up through all the floors, and communicates the power to the stones on the middle floor and the cleaning machine at the top. The power is produced by the weight of water falling on the floats of the wheel. The floats may be either plain, or cased on one edge to hold more weight of water. The wheel may be set to work either way ; the commonest undershot wheel moves towards the water supply ; it is the more usual because it works with a lower fall ; the overshot wheel works away from the head of water, the leat which feeds it passing over the top of the wheel and falling on the floats on the further side.

In everything connected with the old mill there is a sense of wonder and mystery ; the muffled roar and rumble of the old-time machinery, the vibration of the whole structure and the dim light of the several floors, all suggest the steady working of some beneficent monster. Then there is the excellent smell and the harmonious colouring of everything, lightly coated with the mealy dust. Then, again, to go into one of these old mills gives a sense of being in close touch with a thing that has gone on unchanged throughout the centuries, for a water flour mill three or four hundred years ago would have presented the same general features, the same sound, the same good smell, the same mealy coating.

The ancient dovecotes or pigeon houses may well be mentioned in some kind of connection with the flour mills, for they too are no longer in general use. The more important and strongly built ones still remain and

159

FIG. 212.—AN OLD SUSSEX WATERMILL.

FIG. 211.—POST MILL AT BLEDLOW RIDGE,
CHILTERN HILLS, NOW DESTROYED.

FIG. 214.—A TOWER MILL, OCKLEY, SURREY.

FIG. 213.—THE MILL, IBSTONE, BUCKINGHAMSHIRE.

FIG. 215.—A POST MILL, GREAT MILTON, OXFORDSHIRE.

FIG. 216.—BARN AND DOVECOTE, HURLEY-ON-THAMES.

FIG. 217.—FARNHAM, SURREY.

are admirable examples of fitness of purpose. There may be some in actual use and one wonders why they have ever been neglected, for the young birds of six weeks old are a prize in the kitchen, and though the pigeon only hatches out two eggs at a time, yet she produces several broods in the year. The old pigeon houses of circular form, such as that in Fig. 216, had an ingenious way of getting at the nests which were in several rows of niches all the way round the inside of the wall. In the centre was a stout pole pivoted at top and bottom. It had two arms reaching out towards the sides, one near the floor and the other a little way below the level of the upper nesting places ; these held a ladder by which any nest could easily be reached.

They were not all round, for many were square or oblong in plan ; some of the square pattern are charming little buildings with a gable to each face. Others have one continuous ridge and two gables only, and the edges of these are crow-stepped for the more convenient alighting of the birds. One cannot help thinking how delightful such small buildings as the dovecote of the four-gabled pattern would be at the four angles of a walled kitchen garden, and how useful : one for its own purpose, another as an apple room, a third as a root store, and the fourth as a tea house, or any of them for the many storage needs of the garden.

XIII.

ROADS, CARRIAGES, CARTS, AND WAGGONS.

WE who live in a time when there are so many means of communication can hardly realise the state of things that existed in the early
days of the nineteenth century. Roads there were, of a sort, but they
were so inadequately made and so badly kept that a highway of those
days would be barely equal to a third class road of the present time.
All communication by wheeled traffic was slow and difficult and beset
by danger, not only from the state of the road itself, but from attacks
by highwaymen and footpads. Even close to London it was no better,
for we read in a book* published near 1822 :—" There are old persons
who are said to recollect when passengers used to breakfast at
Knightsbridge, dine at Hounslow, and after a day's prodigious exertion,
sup at Staines." In the year 1754 a " flying " coach was announced
and the advertisement stated that however incredible it might appear,
it would certainly arrive in London in four and a half days after leaving
Manchester ! But these flying coaches never made a better pace than
five miles an hour at most.

The ruts in the roads were so deep that it was a common thing for
a private coach to sink into them in mud and water up to the axles,
and even deeper, for though they were hung high it happened not
infrequently that the body of the carriage actually rested on the ground.
Stout bars were carried, to be used as levers for raising the wheels. The
ornamental staves held by the two footmen who stood on a footboard
at the back of state coaches were no doubt a survival of these more
practical implements. Some persons, still living about 1825, could
remember when Piccadilly was a road only—without any foot pave-
ments—and often a very deeply-rutted one. In some places, especially
in the north, there was a line of rough paving stones laid along the middle
of the road for a footway ; it was called the " crown of the causeway."

---

* Pyne's " Microcosm."

Roads were so bad in the middle of the seventeenth century that it took four days to travel by coach from London to Dover, although the road was considered the best in England. At the same time there were stage waggons that carried passengers and a limited amount of light goods. They went twice a week between London and Liverpool and were ten days on the road ; and it took a week to travel from London to York.

There are records of toll bars having been put up as early as in the thirteenth century, and of acts for the repair of highways being passed in 1524 and 1555, to be followed by others in later reigns. Toll-gates or turnpikes (Fig. 235) were set up in the middle of the seventeenth century, but no really sound roads such as we now know were made till in 1818 London McAdam's method of construction was adopted, and the first roads with good foundation of larger, and surface metalling of smaller stone, were built. At the same time care was taken to secure better grading and to make the road not flat but curved a little upward to the crown, also to provide side gullies to secure good drainage, and ditches a few feet away from the edge of the road. This good road builder's name has passed into the language as a verb, and the macadamized road has continued in use to the present day, only varied in recent years by the tarring processes made desirable by the needs of mechanical traffic. There has also been an advance in the quick consolidation of the newly made or repaired road by the use of the powerful steam roller.

Pack horses were used in remote and hilly districts and the only other means of transport besides the road waggons was by barge on the inland waterways (see Fig. 219). Much building was going on in London in the early nineteenth century, and heavy materials, such as bricks, lime and sand, were conveyed in barges such as those shown on page 165, also manure for market gardens and hay and straw for horses. While nearly all the more pictorial of the older means of transport has passed away, the great hay barges of the Thames still remain to us ; their dignified and apparently deliberate movement giving a pleasant reminder of the quiet, restful days of our forefathers of three generations ago

With the improvement of the roads about the year 1820, we hear of a largely increasing number of stage coaches. The earliest on distinct record was as far back as 1634, though possibly some sort of coach may have been introduced nearly a century earlier. The coach of 1634 ran between London and Hackney, hence the name Hackney coach that came into general use for public carriages plying elsewhere. In 1637 there were fifty Hackney coaches; in 1771 there were a thousand.

In the early years of the nineteenth century we also hear that one-horse chaises were in frequent use. About the year 1825 private people travelled either in hired post-chaises or in their own coaches, the more adventurous taking them across to France for a prolonged continental tour. These travelling carriages were for post horses only, there was no coachman's seat (see illustration, Fig. 222). The closed body seated two persons only. It was hung high on large C springs and had a heavy perch that connected the hind wheels with the simple mechanism that allowed the front wheels to lock under. Wide leather slings passed under the body from back to front, so hanging it on the springs, and leather straps were fastened from the tops of the springs diagonally upwards to the body, both back and front, to check the swaying fore and aft. There was no step ; the body was raised so high that three steps at least would have been needed and any fixed step would have been in danger of dragging into the ground when the wheels went down into deep ruts. As gentlemen carried swords there was a horizontal receptacle above the shoulders of the travellers whose form showed outside as a long bulge ; above it was a small oval light. The usual one-horse carriage was a two-wheeled gig with a high chair-like seat.

When Hackney coaches were first brought into use in London there was a great outcry among tradesmen, business people, and the inhabitants generally on account of the noise and disturbance—what would they have said to our modern conditions ? The Thames watermen joined in the complaint on the ground that the coaches occasioned an unfair competition with their business. But in spite of all opposition the coaches multiplied, and by the middle of the eighteenth century their presence was accepted and the protests ceased.

Early in the nineteenth century our roads must have been full of life and interest, with people of all degrees riding—how seldom, except in the wilder south-west, does one now see a ridden horse ?—the many passenger coaches, post-chaises, and private carriages ; the great road waggons ; the farmers taking their produce to market and the travelling traders. The road was a kind of world in itself, full of personal incident and human story. Now nearly all this is swept away ; much that went by road is now carried by rail and the roads are rendered offensive and unsightly by the petrol traffic and its needs. Our roadsides, formerly beautiful with wild flowers and grasses, are now defiled with heaps of rank smelling tarred stones and collections of empty tar barrels, the roads themselves are offensive with a half-stifling reek of tar, and their edges are harshly defined by a pitiless line of cement blocks. So much for our modern improvements ; everything for haste and hurry—nothing for peace and quiet enjoyment and use of life. Surely there was truth in the mouth of the wise man who said we were " progressing backward."

The comfortable wayside inns in towns and villages were the scenes of much life and interest, and it is to be hoped that the quite modern revival of road traffic may restore them to something like their former efficiency. The traveller must have been gratified when he saw not only the swinging sign of his desired haven, but its not unusual accompaniment of well designed and well wrought cresting, surmounting and decorating the horizontal bar from which the actual sign hung, as in the illustration (Fig. 224). Some of these fine iron ornaments remain and are the more treasured now that with hardly any exception the result of modern road conditions is to make everything ugly that formerly was acceptably gracious if not actually beautiful. Even the old wooden signposts are disappearing and are being replaced by iron ones of displeasing form, while already every main road and many lesser ones are disfigured by the unsightly needs of the telegraph and telephone.

The high roads must indeed have been full of lively scene and interesting incident in the opening years of the nineteenth century, for nearly the whole transport of merchandise and consumable supplies had to pass along them. What is now conveyed by rail was then carried in the great road waggons as shown in Fig 218, with wheels so broad that they had to be shod with a double range of five or six-inch tires bolted on in sections. The great width and strength of wheel was made necessary by the bad state of the roads and by the ponderous weight of goods carried in the waggon. The loading was an art in itself, for there must be no danger of the load shifting or jumping from the bumping of the waggon. As the packing went on and when all was finished it was secured by ropes passed across and across and hauled up rigidly tight by two or three men operating a powerful lever.

The road waggons only came into use in the later years of the eighteenth century. A writer of about the date 1801 speaks of them, and with them of gentlemen's carriages and stage coaches, as of something of quite recent introduction. About the year 1820 there were old men still living who remembered when goods were practically, if not wholly, conveyed on pack horses.

Waggons had been in use on farms from an earlier date. There was a lively controversy as to which was the better for farm use, the four-wheeled waggon or the long, heavy two-wheeled cart. In the north, on the banks of the Tweed, where it was considered that the best farming was practised, the two-wheeled cart had the preference, and with its long fore and tail ladders was made to carry as much as a waggon, though the loading, for good balance, had to be more carefully considered. These carts must have been much the same as the long, heavy two-wheeled ones that are still commonly used in France.

The farm waggons could not always keep to the main roads, and the lesser roads were for the most part not wide enough for two to pass. This was one reason for the wearing of the latten bells on the collars of the team, for they were not only a part of the decorative pageantry of farm life, to be displayed along the main roads or on market days, but also served as a warning to carters to stop before entering the lane or at some possible passing place, when another waggon was heard coming from the opposite direction. There is an old legend in West Surrey about two obstinate carters who heard the signal but would not heed it. They met in the lane where it was impossible to pass and as there was no way out they had a fight. How the waggons and horses were got out we are not told. A loaded waggon often got " stood " in a lane in deep mud and could only be got out by hitching on another friendly team. The main roads were but little better a hundred years ago, for we are told that when a load of coal was wanted for a gentleman's country house six miles from Poole, the carter starting at earliest summer daylight and, loading at Poole, only got home late at night.

The general invasion of mechanical transport has robbed us of so much that is of interest and comeliness on the road that it is well to treasure the little that is left and the remembrance of that which is already gone. On some cottage kitchen walls there would be a grand display of cart horse ornaments, such as those in Figs. 223, 225 and 226, for these things, other than the latten bells and various finishings of small brass bosses and hearts fixed in the making of the harness, were the carter's property. There were the face pieces of many patterns, the heavy ear bells attached to the headstall, the coloured horse-hair plumes in brass sockets, the brightly coloured rosettes and streamers of woollen braid and the flashing and jingling head ornaments. It was his pride to dress up his team for the market day or for any occasion that took him along the high road. The horses were, and are still, also specially dressed on the occasion of the cart horse parades that take place in London and some of the midland centres. For the passer-by, to see the brightly painted loaded waggon and the team of four grand horses, with the music of their bells, the glitter of their brasses and the colours of their plumes and ribboned rosette, was a perfectly satisfying picture of rural pageantry.   The brasses, round or heart-shaped or of other outline, were called face pieces ; one was buckled into the bridle front and showed on the horse's forehead.   This was the original place and follows the ancient tradition, for in far away times the brass ornament worn on the horse's forehead was an amulet, such as has been used on horse equipment throughout the ages.   One of the best known patterns of facepiece is the combination of three crescents ; exactly the same design is on the harness of the horses in the Assyrian Room in the British Museum.   The brasses of our waggon teams were placed, not on the head only, but a whole row of them, fastened to a wide leather strap, hung from the collar, others from the martingale, the back band and over the withers.   These brass ornaments, when a large number of them are brought together, show several distinct types.   Among the oldest are those of crescent form ; in the case of the single crescent with the round side down.   Some of the finest of these are not flat but have a raised ridge or keel, and others whether flat or raised, may have a smaller ornament filling the middle space.   The pattern with three crescents has their backs joined, and rather rarely one may see one hanging by the back with the two horns free.   Then there is a whole range of round brasses with ornament of circular perforations of varying sizes, sometimes arranged concentrically and sometimes radiating, and others with perforated patterns in great variety with a basis of heart or star form, cross or fleur-de-lis.   One type shows animal forms ; in the case of heads alone not very good as ornament, but better when they approach heraldic treatment, as of a stag passant, a lion rampant, or the prancing horse of Kent.   Another type shows badges of trades : the barrel of the brewer, the churn of the dairyman, or the anchor of the dock team.   Though the greater number are circular there are some that are of a different form—wide at the shoulder and generally with some kind of heart-shaped base.   Among the round ones there are some that are quite plain and flat that flash finely in sunlight, and others without perforation, but with a plain round central boss ; others again show raised concentric ridges either plain or roped or beaded, leading to a smaller raised central projection.

A special study of these brasses has been made by Miss Eckenstein, who owns a large collection.   In her exhaustive treatise, published in the " Reliquary and Illustrated Archæologist," we read the whole history of their origin and use.

There are also several forms of brass ornament made of a flat disk hinged to the inside top of a circular frame that stood upright on a short leg fixed in the top of the headband, as an alternative to the three-tiered plume of coloured horse hair. They were called fly-terrets. The brass disk swung and flashed with every movement ; another form of head ornament has little bells that jingle prettily.

But the latten bells were the glory of the dressed team. The word latten is from the French *laiton*—brass or bronze. The illustration shows how the bells were set under a leather hood ; the long spikes fitted down in the collar, along the hames. The hood was usually ornamented with a running pattern of ears of corn incised in the leather, and under its edges was a red worsted fringe that partly covered the bells. There were four sets of bells, four bells in each ring, except in the case of the largest bells, in which there were three. Each ring made its own chord and the whole were tuned into one harmony. Though the latten bells had developed into an important ornament, their original function to sound a warning at the entrance of some narrow country road has been earlier referred to.

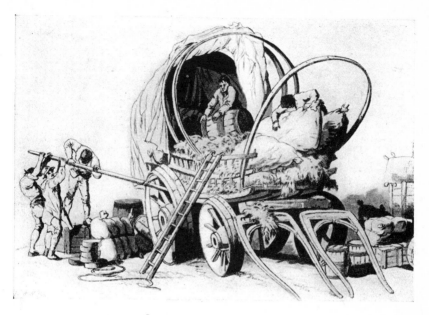

FIG. 218.—LOADING A ROAD WAGGON.

FIG. 219.—BARGES.

From Aquatints by J. B. Pyne.

FIG. 220.—PACK-HORSES.

FIG. 221.—A TWO-WHEEL FARM CART.

FIG. 222.—TRAVELLING CARRIAGE.

From Aquatints by J. B. Pyne.

FIG. 223—THE CARTER'S TROPHY OF HORSE ORNAMENTS.

FIG. 224—SIGN CRESTING, "THE BLACK LION," WATLINGTON,
OXFORDSHIRE.

FIGS. 225 AND 226.—AT THE CART-HORSE PARADE.

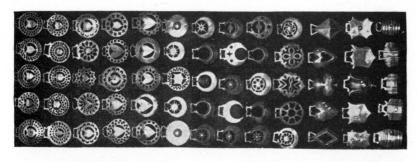

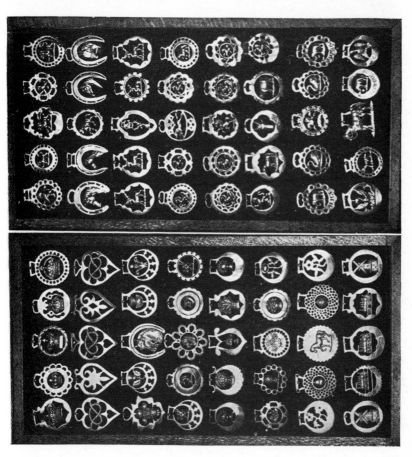

FIGS. 227-229.—A COLLECTION OF FACE-PIECES.

FIG. 232.—BELLS AND
FLY TERRETS.

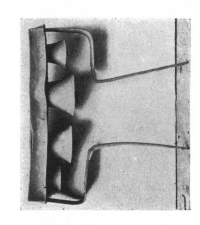

FIG. 233.—LATTEN BELLS.

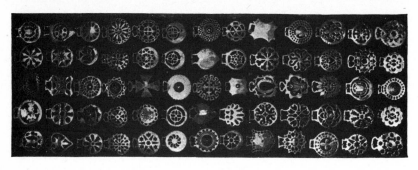

FIGS. 230 AND 231.—FACE-PIECES.

FIG. 234.—TAPROOM OF A COUNTRY INN.
From a Sketch by Thomas Silson, 1837.

FIG. 235.—THE TOLLGATE.

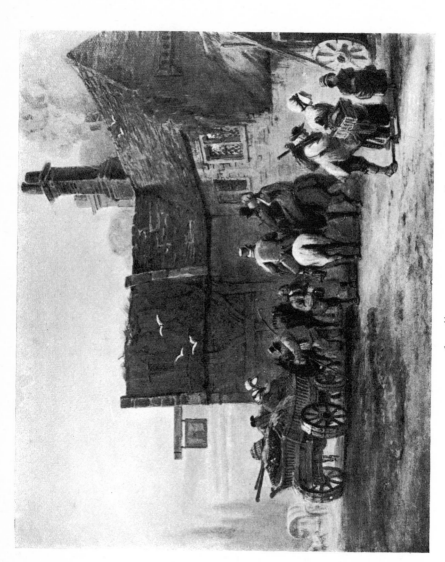

FIG. 236.—" OUTSIDE THE INN."

From the Painting by Luke Clennel.

XIV.

ROADSIDES, GATES AND FENCES.

IS there any North European land that can show the traveller so much charm and beauty on country roads as our dear England, or any such diversity of beauty ?   In the home counties alone there may be first a great stretch of moorland with its own wide horizon, its fresh, perfumed air and its clothing of heath and bracken, gorse and whortle-berry.   Then the scene changes as the road leaves the upland wild and trends downward towards the alluvial soil of the wide valley, with its arable lands and rich pastures. Between the two the road passes between banks of hard sand or crumbling sandstone and is shaped and sheltered by oak and hazel, with an upper fern fringing of Polypody. In a high bank in wild ground is a partly ruined little building, with a low arched opening facing the road.   The stranger wonders what it is, scrambles up the bank and examines the top.   There is nothing but a wide circular opening.   It is an old lime kiln, of which there are many in South-west Surrey, in the sandy region lying between the ridge of chalk that runs east and west through the northern half of the county and the stiff soil of the Weald of Sussex that bounds it on the south. The farm waggons would go loaded with produce to the market at Guildford in the chalk ridge and come home with a load of chalk for the kiln.   Near the kiln there was usually a piece of rough ground where gorse was specially grown for burning the chalk to make the lime that was wanted to correct the acidity of the light land.   The kilns were always built in a bank, so that the chalk could be drawn up above and unloaded close to the opening. The road passes on and then, with a high bank to the left, is at the entrance of a village. A stream runs through the bottom of the valley, and passing over the bridge we see its fringe of pollarded willows.

Those who are in sympathy with plant life will note with pleasure the characteristic growths of the wayside.   Where the chalk is quarried the hedges and roadside wastes are wreathed with the wild Clematis—Travellers' Joy ; then will be bushes of black-berried privet and of red-berried Wayfaring tree, and of white-beam with leaves silver-backed, and in the roadside turf blue Succory and the little yellow rock rose. On the moorland there are the three ordinary kinds of heath and stretches of green bracken, and in the driest parts a close clothing of Whortleberry, well known to the village children who call the little fruits " hurts," and on the roadside, fringes of Wood Germander, a plant of good tonic property, and Harebells in profusion. And for those who look closely, those lovely lowly plants, Eyebright and Milkwort, the tiny Sheeps-bit Scabious, the yellow Tormentil and, perhaps, some tangles of the curious parasitic Dodder. Then in the lanes, Foxgloves and tall purple bellflowers, and in the earlier year glimpses into copses of Bluebells and Primroses. When the road touches the Wealden clay its presence may be known by the pretty patches of silver weed and the yellow stars of fleabane, and the greater abundance of wild roses in the hedgerows. In fact, in any part of the country, anyone who has a fair acquaintance with wild plants could tell the nature of the soil by the wild wayside flowers.

There is no better fence, other than a planted hedgebank, than the old English post and rail, as shown in Fig. 242, and yet how seldom does one see it put up new. On every estate of moderate extent there are oaks to spare, and the woodmen of the country know how to convert them into the proper size and shape. It is good to see a handy man at this work. His tools are his axe, a bittle and a set of three iron wedges. When the tree is down he holds one of the wedges to the butt and gives it a few taps with the back of the axe. It may fly out backwards once or twice, but soon it holds and then he drives it in with full strokes of the axe or bittle ; many woodmen use the axe alone. The bittle is a heavy wooden mallet with a handle a little longer than that of the axe. Its head is a bit of tough apple wood, shod at each end with a tight-fitting iron ring to keep it from splitting. After a few strokes, as the wedge goes in the oak begins to rend, with a sound between a crack and a screech. When one wedge is driven in up to its head another is put in beside it ; by the time this is also buried up to its head the woodman looks out a tough branch and cuts a wooden wedge rather larger than the iron ones. This goes in with them, and with a few more strokes and a continued grieving and straining of the opening fibres, the iron wedges are liberated and are put in nearer the edge. So the work goes on, till the trunk is nearly in halves, only hanging together by some sheets of tough fibre. These are cut through with the axe and the tree lies cleft in two. The further division is into the roughly squared posts, choosing for them the best parts of the tree, and then the rails. If the trunk is long and straight so as to give a length of eighteen feet it is split full length and divided afterwards, but if less than this it is cross cut to nine feet, the length of the rails. Much of the rail stuff is not quite straight ; when the rails are set in the fence they are put with the camber side up ; this not only looks best but is of stronger resistance to any animal leaning on the top. The posts are mortised right through, the rails are a little thinned and tapered at the ends and are fitted together. There is no nailing. The free ends are passed into the mortises of the next post which is loose in its hole, the hole is then filled and rammed tight. If by any chance a rail is broken and has to be replaced the post hole at one end is opened, a lever is put under the foot of the post, and as it is prised up the rails drop out. One does not understand why these capital fences were ever given up and replaced by unsightly ones of iron. An oak fence will stand for half a century without needing any attention ; it costs nothing but the labour to fell and rend the trees, and is always a pleasure to look at. The iron may last longer but it is costly at the beginning and if it is to be kept in proper order it must have a coat of paint or tar varnish, a matter of long labour, every few years ; and it is an everlasting eyesore.

It would be difficult to find a piece of outdoor gear more perfectly fitted for its place and purpose than the old pattern of five-barred gate of the English Southern and Home Counties. It combines all the good qualities of the other hand-wrought appurtenances of our forefathers, so few of which still remain to us, such as the simple and solid domestic furniture of farm and cottage, made of good English oak, that had often been for hundreds of years in the ownership of the same family, but that has now passed into the hands of antiquity dealers and from them into the possession of persons of another class. So it is with this fine old pattern of field gate (Fig. 241) ; on many estates one sees it replaced with a gate of a cheap pattern that reeks of the steam-saw, and is saturated with some preservative in the hope of giving some length of life to the inferior wood. On others, the well-to-do owner, with no knowledge of, or care for, local tradition, and no doubt with the laudable intention of doing the best he can and of sparing no expense in improving the property, puts up heavy gates of expensive workman-ship, painted white, which need frequent repainting and give a suburban appearance to country that is still essentially rural.

The old five-barred gate, made of thoroughly sound oak by a country carpenter who knows and practises the good traditions, will stand for fifty years without so much as a lick of paint, and will probably wear out two or three pairs of posts; moreover, it harmonises absolutely with the accompanying hedge, and has in itself the comeliness of a thing that is well made and is exactly fitted to its purpose. The making of everything of utility is, or should be, based on common-sense, and when one comes to examine this good old gate, going over it carefully and noting every point in its construction, one cannot but feel that admiration and that contentment of mind that are inspired by any true work of art, whether its purpose or aim be the humblest or the most exalted.

The length of the gate may be anything from 9 feet to 11 feet between the posts; 10 feet may be taken as the average. The hanging post has a thickness of 8 inches by 8 inches; the shutting post 7 inches by 7 inches. The posts stand an inch or two higher than the tops of the gate, and both these and the tops of the posts are rounded to throw off the wet. The gate, as to its vertical parts, consists of the "hur" (this is the local word), 5 inches by 3 inches, to which the hinges are bolted; the head, 3 inches by 2½ inches at the shutting end, and the three downrights, 3 inches by three-quarters of an inch, at even distances between. The horizontal and other parts are: At the top, the rail, 3 inches thick and 5 inches deep at the hinge end, thinning to 3 inches at the shutting end; the five spleats 3 inches by three-quarters of an inch, and the diagonal brace. It is put together with wooden pins and iron bolts and nails. It will be seen that the main framework of the gate is formed by the hur, the top rail and the brace. The brace is the only part that varies in shape, for sometimes it is straight and at others it is hollow above, or is cambered; but it is always fixed at the ends in approximately the same places and in the same manner—in a mortise with a tenon and wooden pin. The form of brace shown is rather the best looking, but in any case it should follow the natural line of structure of the wood. Except that the lowest spleat is mortised and pinned, and so keeps the head in position, the remainder is only filling. The brace gives the rigidity to the structure. The spleats are mortised in at the ends, and it is worth noticing, as a point of wise economy of labour, that whereas all are mortised, only two, the lowest and middle ones, are pinned.

Having secured strength, the carpenter lightens the gate by chamfering wherever possible. Here, again, common-sense makes for beauty, for it looks as if it was done intentionally for ornament. Everyone must have noticed the same thing in the rich chamfering of the body parts of a farm waggon. But the chamfered edges not only lighten the gate and look well, but they also present dull surfaces instead of sharp edges to any rough treatment that the gate may have to endure.

FIG. 237.—A SANDY LANE, FITTLEWORTH, SUSSEX.

FIG. 238.—A WEST SURREY LIME KILN.

FIG. 239.—NEAR THE VILLAGE.

FIG. 240.——WILLOWS BY THE BROOK.

FIG. 242.—POST AND RAIL FENCE.

FIG. 241.—FIVE-BARRED GATE AND OAK FENCE.

It is pretty to see how the chamfers stop in good time for the reception on an unbroken flat of a brace or downright and then go on again. In the case of the downrights the chamfer is stopped at the top, but runs out at the bottom. The one next the hinge end is fixed on the further side and is, therefore, chamfered on that side.

The spleats are nailed on with Kentish hurdle nails; they go through and are clinched. The brace is mortised, and fixed at each end with an iron bolt. The sockets of the hinges drop over strong iron pins, turning on a thick flange at the bottom of the pin. From this, in the upper hinge, a stout rod is bolted right through the post ; the lower pin is not bolted, but has only a spike driven in. It will be seen that the weight of the gate pulls hard on the top hinge, as if to pull it out of the post, but that it would tend to drive the lower one into the post.

The gate may be hung in two ways—either within the posts as in the one shown, or on the face of the posts. When it is hung inside, it shuts against a stop formed of a thick oak lath nailed against the inner side of the post. The latches of the older gates were of wood, usually straight, but not infrequently of a slightly curving form, such as the one shown on the gate and more clearly by a separate diagram. One cannot but admire the fine feeling for movement of line shown by the old craftsman. Looking at the original, one wonders if any trained artist could have drawn a better latch. If any fault can be found in the drawing as shown, let it be set down to want of skill in the transcribing, for the lines of the thing itself are singularly beautiful. The prolonged heel of the latch, beyond the loose bolt on which it works, was for the convenience of riders, the pressure of a foot upon it easily throwing up the latch. Everything else belonging to the fastening was of wood ; the keep that limits its movement, nailed on where it is thinned at top and bottom, and the catch that secures the end of the latch. Both were made of a piece of tough oak, the catch being fixed by fitting tightly into a mortise and then being driven.

The other most usual form of fastening is the iron spring latch. A round iron bar has a knob forged on the top ; the lower third of the bar is hammered to a spring temper and the extreme end is flattened and pierced for a bolt that passes through the head of the gate ; it is further pierced for two nails that keep it upright. The head is fitted with a projecting iron loop that is forged into a double strap to enclose the head and top rail, and the whole is fixed with three bolts. The iron knob pulled back releases the bar from the catch. The catch is shaped on the front so that when the gate swings back, the bar slides along it till it

drops in and catches ; the clanging sound of this is familiar to every
country rider. The drawing of the iron spring latch shows a gate that
shuts against the post.

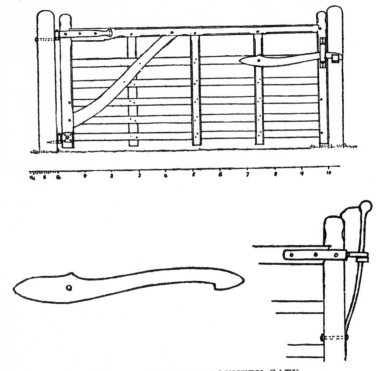

Fig. 243.—A TYPICAL COUNTRY GATE.

This is the form of gate and these are the two typical ways of
fastening common to the country with which I am best acquainted,
namely, the extreme South-west of Surrey and the near adjoining
portions of Sussex and Hampshire. It has a much wider range than this,
and something near it is probably the most usual kind of gate throughout
the greater part of the kingdom.

It is interesting to those who care for etymology to note some of
the names of the several parts of the gate. The " hur " is no doubt
the same word that we have in " hurdle," a pure Anglo-Saxon word.
" Spleat " is allied to " splint " and " splinter," all meaning a piece of
wood divided by splitting. And it is good to observe the accurate shade

FIG. 244.—THE USUAL WOODEN STILE.

FIG. 245.—A DEVONSHIRE STILE, LUSTLEIGH.

FIG. 246.—STILE IN CORNWALL IN SLATE DISTRICT.

FIG. 247.—STILE IN CORNWALL IN SLATE DISTRICT.

of significance in the name "downright" for the vertical pieces that the ordinary observer might rather call uprights. Something upright supposes a firm base from which it springs, whereas here we have a piece of woodwork that hangs from the rail, and that, having its origin and fixing above, is more correctly called a " downright."

The hunting gate is a hand gate, made in all essentials like the foregoing. It measures something near 3 feet 9 inches each way ; it has only one downright, not in the middle but nearer the shutting end. The brace is straight and stretches from near the bottom of the hur to the end of the top rail.

A stile by the roadside is the way into a footpath ; where there is a stile there is a right of way. Sometimes it has two steps, but the single step is more usual. Very different is the kind of stile in stone or slate districts. The massive stone in the Devon stile is typical of the granite that prevails in the regions round Dartmoor (see Figs. 245 and 246) ; and again, typical of the local geological formation are the stiles in the slate districts of Cornwall, sometimes firmly set and sometimes perilously piled, but always showing the simplest ways of adapting the material to the immediate need.

XV.

BRIDGES.

THERE is nothing in the way of simple building that is more full of local character than the old bridges in country districts. Many of those in the home counties are some three hundred years old, and others in the mountainous north and in Wales of still greater antiquity. There are, in South-west Surrey alone, five good old bridges over the small river Wey, all within a part of its flow of only a few miles. They are built of the local Bargate stone. The uneven arches point to the use of some primitive kind of centering, probably an under structure of logs, then of brushwood and a top facing of earth. Some of these bridges have a low parapet wall but the ones shown have the wooden railing of the original pattern, though no doubt several times renewed. It is the best kind of railing for any kind of bridge, whether for road traffic or as a foot-bridge. The horizontal beams, one over each pier and over the crown of each arch, stand out like putlogs and take the brace that supports the post, so that no space is taken up on the road side. In a sixth bridge of the same kind, a few miles further downstream, the true character has been lost by the erection of an iron railing.

It is interesting to observe in the case of all these old bridges, the evidence of a still older ford, made by widening and shallowing the stream and covering the bottom with stones and rough gravel, so that the water is nowhere more than a foot deep and often only a few inches. In fact, in the case of the fine old Eashing bridge, the only road to a part of the works of a paper mill a little way above the bridge is through the river bed. There was grave danger, a few years ago, of this fine old bridge being condemned as unsuitable for modern heavy traffic, but happily it has been saved by becoming the property of the National Trust.

The large bridge at Stopham, in Sussex (see Fig. 249), over the Arun, a few miles north of Arundel, is of more exact architecture. It gains in its appearance of importance from the high central arch, so built to allow the passage of loaded hay barges, and from the small bastion-like projections that come over the pier, for the safety of foot passengers on the narrow road.

FIG. 248.—EASHING BRIDGE, WEST SURREY.

FIG 249.—STOPHAM BRIDGE ON THE ARUN, SUSSEX.

FIG. 250.—A THAMES FOOTBRIDGE.

FIG. 251.—IN THE GWYNANT VALLEY, WALES

FIG. 252.—SWANSIDE BRIDGE, DOWNHAM, LANCASHIRE.

FIG. 253.—WATENDLATH BRIDGE, LAKE DISTRICT.

The many footbridges about the Thames, where a small tributary comes in or where an outfall flows out, are of no particular importance as to structure. The illustration in Fig. 250 shows the weakness of the handrail's support; the small beams that bear the footboards should have been carried out so as to allow of an outer brace to the posts.

The Welsh bridge, as illustrated in Fig. 251, is characteristic of the country and in perfect harmony with the sentiment of the rugged mountainous region and the shallow, rushing river. The large stones that form the piers are built up without mortar and are tied by the rough timbers that are built in with them. Above this is the wooden footway. The whole thing is just right; a more exactly built bridge would have a jarring effect in such a place.

The picture of a stone footbridge at Downham, in Lancashire, on page 190, shows an apparently slight but graceful structure, and reminds one of the wonderful strength of the arch. It is a simple arch and nothing else. There is no walling or anything over the crown to give extra weight and solidity; it is only filled in at each end to let the path pass over easily. It is almost exactly repeated by the bridge at Watendlath, in the near Lake District, shown in Fig. 253, with the same structural influence.

There have been sad losses in recent years of good old bridges that needed repair or renewal, or that have been considered too weak or too narrow for modern traffic. It is not that a good bridge cannot now be built such as will suffice for present needs, but that unfortunately it is rare to find on a rural district council, any member of recognised authority who can influence the decisions of his colleagues towards something of good taste and good tradition as well as sound structure; so it is that we see all over the country the cast-iron engineer's bridge and rarely anything better. A flagrant case occurred not many years since, in the case of a beautiful old town in the Home Counties. The old brick bridge, a single span of good proportion, had been so badly damaged by a heavy flood and the jamming of some floating timber, that it had to be rebuilt. An iron bridge was threatened, but so much concern was felt among the better class of neighbouring residents that a sum amounting to the cost of a new brick bridge, on the lines of the old one, was guaranteed. But the offer was rejected, and the iron bridge, a perpetual eye-sore, was built.

XVI.

SOME OLD-TIME PUNISHMENTS.

A N old instrument of punishment for a shrewish or scolding woman was the ducking stool. The usual form was a wooden chair hung by ropes to the end of a beam that was pivoted on a post at rather less than half its length ; the thicker and longer end of the beam forming an approximate counter-balance to the weight of the chair and the victim. Another form consisted of a long pair of shafts with the chair fixed at one end, a pair of wheels not far from the chair and ropes on the free ends of the shafts for pulling up and down. The arrangement shows that the apparatus was wheeled into the pond or stream, when the release of the shaft end would plunge the chair into the water. It was a rough and barbarous practice that happily went out of use about the middle of the eighteenth century, after a long continuance since Saxon times. Very few wooden ducking stools still exist, but in museums in and near Plymouth there are some well made examples in wrought iron (Figs. 255 and 256). The one with arching top ending in one large hook, is a lesson in good form and fitness for purpose ; the play of line in the arching uprights continued down into the splaying legs, and the scroll work at the back, both show good drawing and proper structural ornament. The other example with straight legs has also some useful scroll ornament in strap iron. In this, the stool was suspended by ropes fastened to the loops at the top of the uprights, that are a vertical continuation of the legs, and no doubt by a third rope at the back. In both there is ample opportunity for tying the person to be punished into the chair. There are cases on record where popular indignation inflicted such severe and prolonged ducking that the offender was actually drowned.

Another instrument used for the same purpose, but that did not involve a ducking, was an arrangement of iron hoops that passed over and round the head, the front partly covering the mouth, with an iron loop or bit that was passed into the mouth and held the tongue down, so forming a complete gag. It was called a brank or scold's bridle, and was in use throughout England and Scotland.

FIG. 254.—THE PILLORY IN THE MARKET-PLACE (POSSIBLY TETSWORTH, GLOUCESTERSHIRE).

From a Water-Colour by Thomas Rowlandson.

FIG. 256.—IRON DUCKING STOOL IN BEAUMONT
PARK MUSEUM, PLYMOUTH.

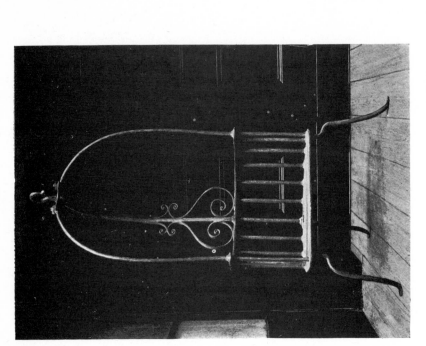

FIG. 255.—IRON DUCKING STOOL IN THE
ATHENÆUM, PLYMOUTH.

The following description of some of these cruel instruments is from an article on "Municipal Punishments of the Middle Ages," by Joseph Stevens, in the "Building News," May 18th, 1883.

"Most forms of brank consist of a kind of helmet or framework of iron, armed with a strong plate or gag to prevent the action of the tongue. They are commonly constructed with hinged side bands, and a hoop which passes over the top of the head and divides in front to give passage to the nose. In applying the instrument the operator stood facing his victim with the expanded bridle in his hand, the gag was then forced into the mouth and the side pieces passed backwards and secured to the cranial band, in some cases by means of a turnbuckle, in others, with a loop and a small padlock. A brank formed on the latter plan, formerly used at Chesterfield, is now in the possession of Sir John Walsham. It bears the initials T.C. and is dated 1688. The person, thus equipped, was paraded through the streets, led by a chain or strap by the constable, beadle or bellman, or, in cases where the culprit refused to walk, was chained to the pillory, whipping-post or market cross, or wheeled in a barrow and submitted to every conceivable insult and degradation from a mob of ruffians.

Fig. 257.—FROM VERNHAM, HAMPSHIRE.

Fig. 258.—FORMERLY AT FARNWORTH, LANCASHIRE.

"A specimen from Vernham, a hamlet in the Upper Test Valley, differs in some particulars from all others I have had an opportunity of inspecting (Fig. 257). It is a helmet composed of open ironwork, formed so as to encase the head down to a level with the neck. The top of the helmet is composed of two bars, which pass from behind forwards, completely over the head and down in front of the face to immediately opposite the mouth, where they terminate in a strong loop. In this loop a tongue-plate, or gag, is made to slide backwards into the mouth and resting on the unruly member, restrains it from being used. It is chiefly in the sliding tongue-plate that this instrument differs from other bridles, the gag being usually fixed to the face-piece. This brank has further a kind of stirrup attached to the tongue-plate, for the reception of a strap or rein, by which the poor gagged creature was paraded about. The base of the stirrup is composed of two bars, one fixing the stirrup to the tongue-plate, while the other is made to act as a lever to the gag, and thus must have furnished the conductor with considerable latitude in inflicting punishment to the mouth. The gag is large and powerful, its length with the slide, being 4½ inches, and its width across the centre 2 inches. In addition to the removable tongue-plate, this instrument differs from other branks in its mode of application ; there being no hinges or openings at the back of the helmet, it must have been forced down on the head from the top.

Fig. 259.—BRANK, FORMERLY AT CHESTERFIELD, DATED 1688.

Fig. 260.—FORMERLY IN READING JAIL.

" Berkshire contains an example of this instrument, a specimen being present in the Reading Jail (Fig. 260). From the imperfect sketch it will be seen that it is not a very severe form. There are holes around the nose-plate, perhaps to relieve the respiration. The gag is not large or thick, and is also pierced with holes, to relieve possibly in some measure the flow of saliva, as suggested by the chaplain of the prison. It has a cushion at the upper part, which it is thought was to relieve the pressure on the vertex of the head. I should imagine, however, that no such humane intention was its object ; but that rather, as the brank is deep it was to prevent the gag from falling below the level of the mouth. The soldier's feather adorning the top, it is conjectured, is a later introduction ; but it more likely implies that the instrument was used to maintain prison discipline in refractory soldiers and others, who must have been frequently incarcerated in the prison for desertion and similar offences.

"The Journal of the British Archæological Association for June, 1869, contains an account of a bridle which belonged to the township of Farnworth, Lancashire, and which was at one time in the possession of Dr. Kendrick. It consists of a framework of iron bands, the next band having a hinge on either side for the purpose of opening it to admit of the offender's head. The plate which passes over the head splits into two in front of the face to give exit to the nose. This plate is secured behind and in front to the collar ; and the gag is not made to slide, but is rivetted to the collar. A piece of leading chain is still attached.

Fig. 261.
MASK BRIDLE,
DODDINGTON PARK.

"There is a peculiar form of mask bridle, once in the possession of Colonel Jarvis, of Doddington Park, Lincolnshire. It has apertures for the eyes, a prominence to fit the nose and a large funnel-shaped peak projecting from the mouth."

A brank in the Ashmolean Museum at Oxford still has the chain by which the person under punishment was dragged through the streets.

For unruly male offenders there was the village lock-up, or cage, a cheerless cell about 8 feet square whose only light and ventilation was afforded by some holes in the upper part of the heavy bolt-studded door. In this Dorset example (illustrated in Fig. 262) the inscription records that it was "erected for the Prevention of Vice and Immorality by Friends of Religion and Good Works, A.D. 1803."

Stocks were set up in every parish ; usually near the church. The person to be punished sat on a bench and his legs were held horizontally by the openings in the thick, heavy boards that formed the instrument of correction. The upper board was hinged at one end and held by an iron loop and staple at the other, where it was secured by a padlock (see Figs. 264, 265, 266). It was usual for the stocks to have a raised post at one or both ends ; this was the whipping post (see Fig. 263) ; it was provided with iron loops near the top for securing the wrists. The harsh treatment of vagrants and other homeless poor is thus described in Chambers's " Book of Days " : " Three centuries ago the flagellation of vagrants and similar characters for slight offences was carried to a cruel extent. Owing to the dissolution of the monasteries, where the poor had chiefly found relief, a vast number of infirm and unemployed persons were suddenly thrown on the country without any legitimate means of support. These destitute persons were naturally led to wander from place to place, seeking a subsistence from the casual alms of any benevolent persons they might chance to meet. Their roving and precarious life soon produced its natural fruits and these again produced severe measures of repression. By an Act passed in '22, Henry VIII., vagrants were to be ' carried to some market town or other place, and there tied to the end of a cart naked and beaten with whips throughout such market town.' Still, vagrancy not only continued but increased, so that several benches of magistrates issued special orders for the apprehension and punishment of vagrants found in their respective districts." The unreasoning cruelty of the times extended to such a degree that there are records of the whipping of persons who were insane and of others who were suffering from small-pox.

The pillory was a form of punishment of great antiquity and of equal barbarity ; like the stocks, it consisted of apertures in a heavy boarded erection (see Fig. 254), but for the head and hands. It seems to have existed in England from the Conquest onwards and was only abolished by an Act of Parliament as lately as the year 1837—not a hundred years ago.

FIG 262.—A DORSET LOCKUP.

FIG. 263.—IRON WHIPPING POST.

FIG. 264.—THE STOCKS, STOW-ON-THE-WOLD.

206

FIG. 265.—INTERIOR OF AN OLD COUNTRY CHURCH.

From the Painting by W. H. Hun

XVII.

THE CHURCH AND CHURCHYARDS

THE passing of time that has brought with it so many changes, nearly all of them to the detriment, if not destruction, of simple beauty, has not spared our churchyards. We no longer see, put up to the memory of our dead, the beautiful old headstones (Figs. 266–268), their upper portion handsomely carved, such as were usual throughout the eighteenth century. Whether the design had for its predominant feature the skull and cross-bones as a reminder of earthly mortality, or the more hopeful heads of cherubs with their accompanying scroll work or foliage, these enrichments gave the stones much dignity, and enough ornament to make them individually interesting. One hardly ever sees two alike, whereas in our present day churchyards there is a wearisome multiplication of the cheap white marble crosses that are made by the hundred in Italy for the English trade. Then the older headstones were of considerable thickness, in pleasant contrast to those that followed in the first half of the nineteenth century when they became tall and thin. It should be more generally known, as it is already well known to architects, that marble is not a good material for monuments in the English climate. Our own Portland stone, good alike in simple design or with sculptured ornament, cannot be beaten for enduring memorials, while there are throughout England many quarries of hard stones suitable for local use.

Then, throughout the eighteenth and into the first decades of the nineteenth centuries, there were the fine altar tombs, as shown in Fig. 270, designed by capable architects, as well as others of a different form and good proportions, often surmounted by an urn. The graves of the poorer folk were marked by the painted wooden grave boards (see Fig. 269), on two end posts with shaped finials. These went out of use, with much else of good old tradition, a little after the middle of the nineteenth century.

The entrance to the churchyard gains in dignity by the presence of the roofed lichgate (see Figs. 271 and 272), whose original purpose was to be a place where the coffin might rest while awaiting the escort of the priest on its way into the church. Formerly there was a stone, called the lich-stone, on which it actually rested. The gate was protected by a solid timber structure, roofed with tile or stone. It is worth observing that the general design of the lichgate follows one of two forms. In the one case the ridge of the roof runs the same way as the path, and a gable faces the spectator ; in the other the ridge runs across the path, when the form becomes that of a shed, with the level line of the eaves facing those who approach. In both cases the ancient examples, standing, as they generally do, detached and unsupported by anything near, show good treatment of timber in accordance with structural necessity. The building of lichgates has been revived and many new examples of good design may be seen.

It is rare to find now an ancient country church that has not been restored within the last sixty to eighty years. One cannot but applaud the action of those who had the commendable desire to have their place of worship in a sound and seemly condition, and the old, deep panel-walled pews are not to be regretted ; yet so much has been done that is deplorable, especially in the earlier years of the Restoration period, that it is quite a pleasure to find an old church as yet untouched and full of the unaltered memory of the humble worship of many generations. The danger of injudicious restoration has now passed, for advice may readily be had from the Society for the Protection of Ancient Buildings, and there are architects of the highest repute whose work of restoration is entirely beneficial.

A growing evil, rampant within the last forty years, is now happily being checked by the good sense of the more enlightened incumbents. This is the placing on graves of artificial wreaths covered with glasses. It is no matter of surprise that they should have become popular with uneducated people, for the things have a certain meretricious prettiness when displayed in the shop windows of funeral furnishers. But when placed in the churchyard, the round glass becomes offensively conspicuous, glaring and flashing in all parts of the sacred ground and entirely destroying its proper attributes of dignity, peace and restfulness. Now, in many places they are, and soon, let us hope, in all, they will be entirely forbidden.

In some churches in the Midlands there still remain the relics of a pretty old custom, that of carrying garlands at the funerals of young girls.

The word garland usually means a hanging wreath, but these, called maidens' garlands, were not of flowers and leaves but quite

FIGS. 266-268.—TYPICAL EIGHTEENTH
CENTURY HEADSTONES.

FIG. 269.—GRAVE BOARDS.

FIG. 270.—ALTAR TOMBS.

FIG. 272.—A TIMBER LYCHGATE, MONNINGTON-ON-
WYE, HEREFORDSHIRE.

FIG. 271.—LYCHGATE, PULBOROUGH, SUSSEX.

FIG. 274.—LLANWRCHWYN, WALES.

FIG. 275.—SLAPTON, NORTHAMPTONSHIRE.

Fig. 273.—THE LICHGATE, ISLEHAM, CAMBRIDGESHIRE.

artificial. They were made on a framework of two flat wooden hoops, one above the other, connected by several uprights that bent over and joined at the top. This was covered with coloured paper, and had paper or ribbon rosettes of many colours at intersecting points. Near the top, where the framework began to arch over, a horizontal band, richly decorated with rosettes, ran right round, with another of the same near the bottom. Streamers of ribbon or ornamented paper came from the top, passed under the shoulder band and then hung free to a little below the base of the garland. There were two loops at the top, one outside for hanging it up and one within from which was suspended a piece of paper or other material, sometimes shaped like a glove, on which was written the girl's name and date of death, sometimes with the addition of a verse of pious sentiment. The illustration in Fig. 277 shows two of these garlands in the church at Ilam, in Staffordshire. They are without the streamers which have probably become detached with age, and they are hung in a rather unusual manner under a stone arch; they were more commonly suspended from the lower part of the woodwork of the roof, from which they would hang more easily. In some cases they were placed over the dead girl's seat.

II

This old custom remained longest in force in Derbyshire, and within the last fifty years there were at least a dozen churches in that county in which they were still to be seen. At Heanor, where there were a large number, they were done away with when a new incumbent gave the church a thorough cleaning. Even in earlier centuries they were not always favoured by the higher powers, for we read in Dr. Cox's " Churches of Derbyshire " about a Bishop of Ely, on the occasion of a visitation in the year 1662, who condemned them as " childish gew-gaws . . .hung where they hinder the prospect or until they grow foul and dusty, withered and rotten." One cannot but sympathise with the good bishop's deprecation of a quantity of meretricious ornament being hung in the church, for even within living memory as many as fifty remained in one Midland place ; but at the present day, when we justly prize all record and example of antiquarian interest, the small remaining number of evidences of an age-long custom of affectionate piety, may well be honoured by being retained in their original places.

That the custom of hanging maidens' garlands in churches prevailed also in the more southern country, and in all probability throughout the country, we learn from Gilbert White's " Selborne," for in one of his letters describing the antiquities and customs of his parish we read :— " In the middle aisle " (of Selborne Church) " there is nothing remarkable : but I remember when its beams were hung with garlands in honour of young women of the parish, reputed to have died virgins ; and recollect to have seen the clerk's wife cutting, in white paper, the resemblance of gloves, and ribbons to be twisted in knots and roses, to decorate these memorials of chastity. In the church of Faringdon, which is the next parish, many garlands of this sort still remain." The same genial writer, telling us about the recasting of the old church bells, three in number and much out of tune, that were cast into four, to which a fifth, the gift of a local baronet, was added, says :—" The day of the arrival of this tunable peal was observed as a high festival by the village, and rendered more joyous by an order from the donor that the treble bell should be fixed bottom upward in the ground and filled with punch, of which all present were permitted to partake." This was in the year 1735.

The hour glass was commonly in use in churches in the seventeenth century. It had become customary for the clergy to deliver sermons of inordinate length, and the glass was to remind the preacher that he must not protract his discourse beyond the allotted hour. It was usually on the left hand side of the pulpit, standing out in an iron cage or more simple socket, with a bracket of wrought iron, often finely designed. The glass in the illustration (Fig. 276) is not in a parish church but in an almshouse, fixed to the wall of the Lucas Asylum at Wokingham in Berkshire.

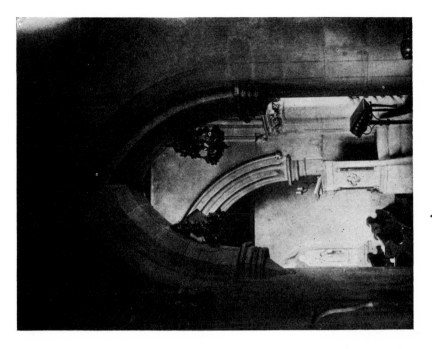

FIG. 277.—MAIDENS' GARLANDS, ILAM, STAFFORDSHIRE.

FIG. 276.—IN THE CHAPEL, LUCAS ASYLUM, WOKINGHAM.

INDEX.